THE RUINS OF POMPEII: A SERIES OF EIGHTEEN PHOTOGRAPHIC VIEWS, WITH AN ACCOUNT OF THE DESTRUCTION OF THE CITY, AND A DESCRIPTION OF THE MOST INTERESTING REMAINS

Published © 2017 Trieste Publishing Pty Ltd

ISBN 9780649136575

The ruins of Pompeii: a series of eighteen photographic views, with an account of the destruction of the city, and a description of the most interesting remains by Thomas H. Dyer

Edited by Trieste Publishing Pty Ltd.
Cover © 2017

www.triestepublishing.com

THOMAS H. DYER

THE RUINS OF POMPEII: A SERIES OF EIGHTEEN PHOTOGRAPHIC VIEWS, WITH AN ACCOUNT OF THE DESTRUCTION OF THE CITY, AND A DESCRIPTION OF THE MOST INTERESTING REMAINS

 Trieste

THE RUINS OF POMPEII.

A SERIES OF EIGHTEEN PHOTOGRAPHIC VIEWS.

WITH AN ACCOUNT OF THE DESTRUCTION OF THE CITY, AND A DESCRIPTION OF THE MOST INTERESTING REMAINS.

BY THOMAS H. DYER, LL.D.

LONDON:

BELL AND DALDY, 186, FLEET STREET,

A. W. BENNETT, BISHOPSGATE STREET.

1867.

PREFACE.

N works like the present the usual practice is reversed—the letter-press is made subservient to the illustrations; and these, especially when they consist of photographs, must be left to the selection of artists. Hence, views may sometimes be chosen for their pictorial effect rather than their fitness to illustrate the subject in hand. Nevertheless, from the necessary truthfulness of photographic pictures, it is hoped that the present volume may, with the aid of some engravings, convey a good general idea of Pompeii.

The substance of much of the letter-press is taken from the well-known work on Pompeii, originally published by the Society for the Diffusion of Entertaining Knowledge, of which the writer of these pages has recently been engaged in preparing a new edition. The aid derived from other sources is acknowledged in the proper places.

LIST OF PHOTOGRAPHS.

RECENT EXCAVATIONS.

THE RUINS OF POMPEII.

HE Photograph which we have inserted by way of frontispiece to this volume, although embracing some of the more
recent excavations, does not offer any very striking or
remarkable object; but it will convey a good idea of the
general appearance of Pompeii. One of its chief characteristics is the numerous isolated pillars, arranged in quadrangular form,
which once supported the roof of an atrium or a peristyle that has now
vanished, though its side walls are still erect. These walls are sometimes
entirely bare of stucco, and display, like those in the foreground of the photograph, the rude materials of which they are constructed; while others, like
those in the middle distance, not only retain their coating of stucco, but also
the designs and ornaments with which it was painted. When these are more
valuable than usual they are protected from the weather by a sort of eaves,
or short projecting roof, being built over them. The distance, with the
modern farm-house and stone-pines, shows parts that have not yet been
excavated; for those ruins that now appear so cleanly emptied were once
filled with a cineritious soil, and above them were fields, and crops, and
trees, and habitations. The nature of the material with which they were
filled has not only served to preserve them, but has also rendered the
excavation of them a comparatively easy task. It is an interesting sight to
watch the clearing of one of these houses. As the pickaxe and shovel
loosen with facility the light dry pumice from the surface of the walls, the
pictures with which they are adorned reveal themselves to us in colours
almost as brilliant as when they were first laid on. As the floor is
approached the interest of the process increases; for it is in the last few

B

feet of the deposit that objects of curiosity or value are discovered, such as furniture, jewellery, human remains, coins, and other objects of the like kind—the last earthly spoils of a generation that existed eighteen centuries ago.

A brief account of the buried city may possibly increase the reader's interest in its fate. Places, as well as persons, attract us by their vicissitudes, and the attraction increases in proportion to our knowledge of their history.

CAMPANIA was, and still is, one of the loveliest and most fertile districts of Italy. The authors of antiquity, Greek as well as Roman, prose writers as well as poets, are loud in their praises of its mild and luxurious climate, its prolific soil, its hospitable sea and excellent harbours. Rome filled her granaries from the plains around Capua; the oil produced at Venafrum, the wines grown on Mount Massicus and in the Falernian vineyards were of a quality so superior that they could be found only on the tables or in the cellars of the rich and great.

Of this delightful region all the charms and attractions seemed to be concentrated, and as it were epitomized, on the shores of the CRATER, as, from its cup-like shape, the ancients called the Bay of Naples. The beauty and fertility of the spot had induced the Greeks to settle there at a very early period. Cumae, one of the earliest colonies of that people in Italy, had been built near the northern extremity of the bay, long, probably, before the foundation of Rome. The shores of the bay now gradually became studded with Greek towns, such as Neapolis, Herculaneum, Pompeii, and others, either independent settlements or colonies of Cumae. After falling successively under the domination of the Etruscans and the Samnites, Campania was finally reduced by Rome. The wealthy and luxurious Romans of the later republic and the empire fully appreciated the charms of the Bay of Naples; its shores formed one of their favourite places of retirement and recreation, and soon became dotted with their magnificent villas.

But all underneath this charming region lay the elements of destruction. Westward of Naples this fact was indeed patent enough, and obvious to the most careless observer. Traces of volcanic action had obtained for the country round Cumae the name of *Campi Phlegraei*, or the burning fields; while the *Solfatara*, near Puteoli, called by Strabo the "Forum of Vulcan," seems to have been in much the same state of activity in the reign of Augustus as it is at the present time. In the same neighbourhood were evident traces of extinct volcanoes. More careful inquirers had even remarked about Vesuvius the evidence of eruptions which must have occurred at a period long antecedent to any historical traditions; and these appearances have been recorded both by Strabo and by Diodorus Siculus. Pompeii was indeed actually built on the lava thrown out by one of these ancient eruptions. But that Vesuvius was a volcanic mountain must have been utterly ignored by the people in general, and even by persons of education; since we find the younger Pliny telling us that those who surveyed from a distance the great eruption of the year 79 could not determine from what mountain it proceeded. So small was their apprehension of having so dangerous a neighbour !

The country in which Pompeii stands appears to have been originally occupied by the Oscans, whose language probably, after a few generations, again prevailed over that of the Greek colonists. As most of the ancient Italian cities claimed some Greek or Trojan hero as their founder, so Pompeii pretended to have been built by Hercules, but without even the etymological pretext which gave some colouring to a like pretension on the part of Herculaneum. All that can be inferred from such claims is that both cities were probably of Greek origin. Respecting some attempts to explain the name of Pompeii we shall be silent, and descend at once from the realms of fiction to those of history.

After the great victory won by the consul Manlius at the foot of Mount Vesuvius in B.C. 340, the Campanians had become more or less subject to or allied with Rome, though always inclined to throw off the yoke. The name of Pompeii itself, however, does not appear in history till B.C. 310, although it must have been in existence some centuries before. At the date just mentioned Pompeii was attacked by P. Cornelius, the commander of a Roman fleet, who, however, was ultimately repulsed. We hear nothing of Pompeii when, after the fatal defeat of the Romans by Hannibal at Cannæ (B.C. 216), the Campanians revolted against Rome; but in the Social, or Marsic, war in B.C. 91, Pompeii played a conspicuous part. This revolt terminated in the final and complete subjection of Campania, and the severe punishment of several of its principal cities. During this war Pompeii was besieged by L. Cornelius Sulla, and it was probably on this occasion that its ancient walls were damaged and partly overthrown. It appears, however, for what reason we know not, to have escaped the hard fate of several of its sister-cities, and even to have been admitted to the Roman franchise. But

Sulla established there a military colony, which, from him and from the patron-goddess of the city, obtained the name of Colonia Veneria Cornelia.

Henceforth Pompeii sank into the condition of a second or third rate municipal town. It was during this period, probably, that many of those temples and public buildings were erected, especially in the Forum and its neighbourhood, which are in the Roman rather than in the Greek style of architecture. The only remains of the latter style that can be confidently pointed to are those of the temple in the Triangular Forum, which must be referred to a time long antecedent to the Roman occupation. The theatres also in its immediate neighbourhood may perhaps have been originally of Greek design, though afterwards altered to suit the Roman fashion. After the reduction of Pompeii, it became, like other towns in that attractive neighbourhood, a favourite resort of wealthy and distinguished Romans ; among whom was Cicero, who had a villa there, which he frequently mentions in his letters. The Emperor Augustus despatched thither a colony, which appears to have been settled outside the Herculanean Gate, in the district of the Street of the Tombs, and to have borne the name of Pagus Augustus Felix. In the year 59, in the reign of the Emperor Nero, an affray took place between the Pompeians and some of the inhabitants of the neighbouring town of Nuceria, who had come to see the gladiatorial combats in the amphitheatre of Pompeii. The Nucerians having been worsted and maltreated, preferred a complaint to the Emperor, who, as we learn from Tacitus, punished the Pompeians by prohibiting all theatrical entertainments in their city for a period of ten years. The truth of history, in this certainly not very important affair, has been confirmed by the discovery of a rude etching on the plaster wall of a house in the Street of Mercury, which, from the inscription scratched in the corner of it, appears to represent the affray in question.

The term of punishment had not half expired when, in A. D. 63, Pompeii and its neighbourhood were visited with a severe earthquake, which inflicted considerable damage on the town. In the following year, another shock occurred at Naples while Nero was displaying his musical talent by singing in the theatre. He had hardly time to leave it before the building fell, and he was thus preserved a few years longer for fresh crimes and a worse fate. These earthquakes were doubtless occasioned by the pent-up fires of Vesuvius, which in a few years were to find a vent at the expense of a still more terrible destruction. The effects of them are still visible at

Pompeii. The mosaic floors of the houses are frequently found to be broken and thrown out of their level; and the extensive repairs which were evidently going on at the time of the final catastrophe can be referred to no other cause.

At length, in A. D. 79, the great eruption broke out to which we have already alluded. The younger Pliny, who was an eye-witness of this catastrophe, has so graphically described it, as well as the death of his uncle, in two letters to the historian Tacitus, that any account of Pompeii in which his description was omitted might be deemed incomplete. It runs as follows in the translation of Melmoth :—

"Your request that I would send you an account of my uncle's death, in order to transmit a more exact relation of it to posterity, deserves my acknowledgments; for, if this accident shall be celebrated by your pen, the glory of it, I am well assured, will be rendered for ever illustrious. And notwithstanding he perished by a misfortune, which, as it involved at the same time a most beautiful country in ruins, and destroyed so many populous cities, seems to promise him an everlasting remembrance, notwithstanding he has himself composed many and lasting works; yet I am persuaded the mentioning of him in your immortal works will greatly contribute to eternize his name. Happy I esteem those to be whom Providence has distinguished with the abilities either of doing such actions as are worthy of being related, or of relating them in a manner worthy of being read; but doubly happy are they who are blessed with both these uncommon talents—in the number of which my uncle, as his own writings and your history will evidently prove, may justly be ranked. It is with extreme willingness, therefore, I execute your commands; and should indeed have claimed the task if you had not enjoined it. He was at that time with the fleet under his command at Misenum. On the 24th of August, about one in the afternoon, my mother desired him to observe a cloud which appeared of a very unusual size and shape. He had just returned from taking the benefit of the sun, and after bathing himself in cold water, and taking a slight repast, was retired to his study. He immediately arose and went out upon an eminence, from whence he might more distinctly view this very uncommon appearance. It was not at that distance discernible from what mountain this cloud issued, but it was found afterwards to ascend from Mount Vesuvius. I cannot give a more exact description of its figure than by resembling it to that of a pine-tree, for it shot up a great height in the form of a trunk, which extended itself at the top into a sort of branches, occasioned, I imagine, either by a sudden gust of air that impelled it, the force of which decreased as it advanced upwards, or the cloud itself, being pressed back again by its own weight, expanded in this manner: it appeared sometimes bright and sometimes dark and spotted, as it was more or less impregnated with earth and cinders. This extraordinary phenomenon excited my uncle's philosophical curiosity to take a nearer view of it. He ordered a light vessel to be got ready, and gave me the liberty, if I thought proper, to attend him. I rather chose to continue my studies; for, as it happened, he had given me an employment of that kind. As he was coming out of the house, he received a note from Rectina, the wife of Bassus, who was in the utmost alarm at the imminent danger which threatened her; for her villa being situated at the foot of Mount Vesuvius, there was no way to escape but by sea: she earnestly entreated him, therefore, to come to her assistance. He accordingly changed his first design, and what he began with a philosophical he pursued with an heroical turn of mind. He ordered the galleys to put to sea, and went himself on board, with an intention of assisting not only Rectina, but several others, for the villas stand extremely thick upon that beautiful coast. When hastening to the place from which others fled with the utmost terror, he steered his course direct to the point of danger, and with so much calmness and presence of mind, as to be able to make and dictate his observations upon the motion and figure of that dreadful scene. He was now so nigh the mountain, that the cinders, which grew thicker and hotter the nearer he approached, fell into the ships, together with pumice-stones and black pieces of burning rock. They were likewise in danger, not only of being aground by the sudden retreat of the sea, but also from the vast fragments which rolled down from the mountain and obstructed all the shore. Here he stopped to consider whether he should return back again; to which the pilot advising him, 'Fortune,' said he, 'befriends the brave; carry me to Pomponianus.' Pomponianus was then at Stabiæ, separated by a gulf, which the sea, after several insensible windings, forms upon the shore. He had already sent his baggage on board; for though he was not at that time in actual danger, yet being within the view of it, and, indeed, extremely near, if it should in the least increase, he was determined to put to sea as soon as the wind should change. It was favourable, however, for carrying my uncle to Pomponianus, whom he found in the greatest consternation. He embraced him with tenderness, encouraging and exhorting him to keep up his spirits, and the more to dissipate his fears, he ordered, with an air of unconcern, the baths to be got ready; when, after having bathed, he sat down to supper with great cheerfulness, or at least (what is equally heroic) with all the appearance of it. In the meanwhile, the eruption from Mount Vesuvius flamed out in several places with much violence, which the darkness of the night contributed to render still more visible and dreadful. But my uncle, in order to soothe the apprehensions of his friend, assured him it was only the burning of the villages, which the country people had abandoned to the flames. After this he retired to rest, and it is most certain he was so little discomposed as to fall into a deep sleep; for being pretty fat, and breathing hard, those who attended without actually heard him snore. The court which led to his apartment being now almost filled with stones and ashes, if he had continued there any time longer, it would have been impossible for him to have made his way out: it was thought proper, therefore, to awaken him. He got up, and went to Pomponianus and the rest of his company, who were not unconcerned enough to think of going to bed. They consulted together whether it would be most prudent to trust to the houses, which now shook from side to side with frequent and violent concussions; or fly to the open fields, where the calcined stones and cinders, though light indeed, yet fell in large showers, and threatened destruction. In this distress they resolved for the fields, as the less dangerous situation of the two; a resolution which, while the rest of the company were hurried into it by their fears, my uncle embraced upon cool and deliberate consideration. They went out then, having pillows tied upon their heads with napkins; and this was their whole defence against the storm of stones that fell around them. It was now day everywhere else, but there a deeper darkness prevailed than in the most obscure night; which, however, was in some degree dissipated by torches and other lights of various kinds. They thought proper to go down further upon the shore, to observe if they might safely put out to sea; but they found the waves still run extremely high and boisterous. There my uncle, having drunk a draught or two of cold water, threw himself down upon a cloth which was spread for him, when immediately the flames, and a strong smell of sulphur, which was the forerunner of them, dispersed the rest of the company, and obliged him to rise. He raised himself up with the assistance of two of his servants, and instantly fell down dead; suffocated, as I conjecture, by some gross and noxious vapour, having always had weak lungs.

and being frequently subject to a difficulty of breathing. As soon as it was light again, which was not till the third day after this melancholy accident, his body was found entire, and without any marks of violence upon it, exactly in the same posture that he fell, and looking more like a man asleep than dead. During all this time, my mother and I, who were at Misenum —but as this has no connection with your history, so your inquiry went no farther than concerning my uncle's death; with that, therefore, I will put an end to my letter. Suffer me only to add, that I have faithfully related to you what I was either an eye-witness of myself, or heard immediately after the accident happened, and before there was time to vary the truth. You will choose out of this narrative such circumstances as shall be most suitable to your purpose; for there is a great difference between what is proper for a letter and a history—between writing to a friend, and writing for the public. Farewell!"

Tacitus having pressed Pliny to send him further particulars, the latter addressed to him a second letter, as follows:—

"The letter which, in compliance with your request, I wrote to you concerning the death of my uncle, has raised, it seems, your curiosity to know what terrors and dangers attended me while I continued at Misenum: for there, I think, the account in my former broke off.

'Though my shocked soul recoils, my tongue shall tell.'

"My uncle having left us, I pursued the studies which prevented my going with him, till it was time to bathe. After which I went to supper, and from thence to bed, where my sleep was greatly broken and disturbed. There had been, for many days before, some shocks of an earthquake, which the less surprised us as they are extremely frequent in Campania; but they were so particularly violent that night, that they not only shook everything about us, but seemed indeed to threaten total destruction. My mother flew to my chamber, where she found me rising, in order to awaken her. We went out into a small court belonging to the house, which separated the sea from the buildings. As I was at that time but eighteen years of age, I know not whether I should call my behaviour, in this dangerous juncture, courage or rashness; but I took up Livy, and amused myself with turning over that author, and even making extracts from him, as if all about me had been in full security. While we were in this posture, a friend of my uncle, who was just come from Spain to pay him a visit, joined us; and observing me sitting by my mother with a book in my hand, greatly condemned her calmness, at the same time that he reproved me for my careless security. Nevertheless, I still went on with my author. Though it was now morning, the light was exceedingly faint and languid; the buildings all around us tottered, and though we stood upon open ground, yet, as the place was narrow and confined, there was no remaining there without certain and great danger: we therefore resolved to quit the town. The people followed us in the utmost consternation; and, as to a mind distracted with terror, every suggestion seems more prudent than its own, pressed in great crowds about us in our way out. Being got at a convenient distance from the houses, we stood still, in the midst of a most dangerous and dreadful scene. The chariots which we had ordered to be drawn out, were so agitated backwards and forwards, though upon the most level ground, that we could not keep them steady, even by supporting them with large stones. The sea seemed to roll back upon itself, and to be driven from its banks by the convulsive motion of the earth: it is certain at least the shore was considerably enlarged, and several sea animals were left upon it. On the other side a black and dreadful cloud, bursting with an igneous serpentine vapour, darted out a long train of fire, resembling flashes of lightning, but much larger. Upon this our Spanish friend, whom I mentioned above, addressing himself to my mother and me with great warmth and earnestness: 'If your brother and your uncle,' said he, 'is safe, he certainly wishes you may be so too; but if he perish, it was his desire, no doubt, that you might both survive him: why, therefore, do you delay your escape a moment?' We could never think of our own safety, we said, while we were uncertain of his. Hereupon our friend left us, and withdrew from the danger with the utmost precipitation. Soon afterwards the cloud seemed to descend, and cover the whole ocean; as indeed it entirely hid the island of Capreæ and the promontory of Misenum. My mother strongly conjured me to make my escape at any rate, which, as I was young, I might easily do: as for herself, she said, her age and corpulency rendered all attempts of that sort impossible. However she would willingly meet death, if she could have the satisfaction of seeing that she was not the occasion of mine. But I absolutely refused to leave her, and taking her by the hand I led her on: she complied with great reluctance, and not without many reproaches to herself for retarding my flight. The ashes now began to fall upon us, though in no great quantity. I turned my head, and observed behind us a thick smoke, which came rolling after us like a torrent. I proposed, while we had yet any light, to turn out of the high road, lest she should be pressed to death in the dark by the crowd that followed us. We had scarce stepped out of the path, when darkness overspread us, not like that of a cloudy night, or when there is no moon, but of a room when it is shut up and all the lights extinct. Nothing then was to be heard but the shrieks of women, the screams of children, and the cries of men; some calling for their children, others for their parents, others for their husbands, and only distinguishing each other by their voices; one lamenting his own fate, another that of his family; some wishing to die from the very fear of dying; some lifting their hands to the gods; but the greater part imagining that the last and eternal night was come, which was to destroy the gods and the world together. Among these were some who augmented the real terrors by imaginary ones, and made the frighted multitude falsely believe that Misenum was actually in flames. At length a glimmering light appeared, which we imagined to be rather the forerunner of an approaching burst of flames, as in truth it was, than the return of day. However, the fire fell at a distance from us. Then again we were immersed in thick darkness, and a heavy shower of ashes rained upon us, which we were obliged every now and then to shake off, otherwise we should have been crushed and buried in the heap. I might boast that, during all this scene of horror, not a sigh or expression of fear escaped from me, had not my support been founded in that miserable, though strong, consolation—that all mankind were involved in the same calamity, and that I imagined I was perishing with the world itself! At last this dreadful darkness was dissipated by degrees, like a cloud of smoke; the real day returned, and even the sun appeared, though very faintly, and as when an eclipse is coming on. Every object that presented itself to our eyes (which were extremely weakened) seemed changed, being covered over with white ashes, as with a deep snow. We returned to Misenum, where we refreshed ourselves as well as we could, and passed an anxious night between hope and fear—though indeed with a much larger share of the latter—for the earthquake still continued, while several enthusiastic people ran up and down, heightening their own and their friends' calamities by terrible predictions. However, my mother and I, notwithstanding the danger we had passed, and that which still threatened us, had no thoughts of leaving the place till we should receive some account from my uncle.

"And now you will read this narrative without any view of inserting it in your history, of which it is by no means worthy; and indeed you must impute it to your own request if it shall deserve the trouble of a letter. Farewell." *

It will be perceived that Pliny in this description likens the appearance of the eruption to that of a stone-pine, which first shoots up into the air with a lofty column, and then spreads itself out into an expanding head. The ejection of that tall straight column shows the violence and the sudden-ness of the eruption, while the spreading of the head proves that the ejected matter must have been composed of light materials—*lapillo*, or pumice stone, so calcined as to be capable of being supported in some degree by the atmosphere. It was this substance that descended on the doomed towns of Herculaneum, Pompeii, and Stabiæ. It does not appear to have been accompanied with lava. Had the eruption consisted of lava, Pompeii at least would have escaped destruction, as its elevated situation would have preserved it from the fiery stream. The lava that may be seen at Hercula-neum is the produce of subsequent eruptions. The ashes ejected formed a covering over Pompeii upwards of twenty feet in depth. Subsequent erup-tions have added to the deposit a crust of a few feet in depth; but this may be distinguished from the *lapillo* by its colour; for while the original deposit is of a greyish white, the superincumbent layer approaches to black. Rocks and stones were probably also ejected, and after a time streams of wet sand or mud. This seems to have proved as fatal, or even more so, than the *lapillo*; since it is evident that many persons who were escaping on the surface of the *lapillo*, or had taken refuge where it could not penetrate, were overtaken and buried by the mud. Earthquake was another agent in this work of destruction, as is evident from the description of some of the bodies discovered. In one instance a man had been crushed by the falling of a pillar in the Forum, near the temple of Jupiter; and in another several skeletons were discovered of persons overwhelmed by the falling of a wall. However, it is not probable that many were killed in this manner. The deformity produced by the eruption in the external face of nature may well be imagined. Tacitus, in the fourth book of his Annals, and Martial, in one of his epigrams, are vouchers for it. For miles around Vesuvius, that smiling landscape was turned into an arid desert, without a trace of cultiva-tion. Many years must have passed over before it began again to assume

---

* Pliny's Letters, vi. 20 ; Melmoth's translation.

even a surface of verdure; many centuries before the soil recovered any
portion of its ancient fertility.

Scarcely anything more horrible can be imagined than the fate of the
inhabitants of these devoted cities. Of those who escaped destruction,
most must have lost their whole means of subsistence, many probably their
reason also; whilst the death of those who perished must have been of the
most appalling description. They died for our benefit! the hard-hearted
antiquarian may exclaim; they must have died sooner or later, but in no
other way could their death have benefited posterity. They were, as it
were, embalmed for our instruction, sent down to us in the very last acts
of their lives; the sacrifice which they were preparing left incomplete; the
bread which they were baking for their daily food still in the oven; the
drugs which were to correct the high living of their luxurious lives in the
act of being made into pills; the money that was to pay for all these things
still in their purses! Asmodeus, in Le Sage's romance of the "Diable
Boiteux," merely by waving his right arm unroofs all the houses of Madrid,
so that Don Cleofas could look into them as into a pie whose crust has been
removed, and survey all the actions of their inhabitants. Vesuvius has done
us a similar favour, and enabled us to see what the Pompeians were about
eighteen centuries ago! But a city of the dead. True; yet so well preserved that if its inhabitants could be recalled to life they might still
recognize their accustomed haunts, turn mechanically into their familiar
chambers, again use and admire their furniture and their pictures. Thus
a calamity so horrible in its nature has had the singular effect of adding
another charm to the environs of Naples, by embalming the remains of two
ancient cities for the inspection of modern travellers. The general aspect of
the ruins may be gathered from the frontispiece, and will be still further
illustrated by another photograph which we annex, also taken from the more
recent excavations.

It is this that renders a visit to Pompeii so pre-eminently interesting.
Rome, indeed, possesses far more striking and celebrated monuments than
can be found here, and leaves on the spectator a deeper sense of imperial
grandeur. None but a people-king, the sovereign of the greater part of the
known world, could have reared the Colosseum, or have lined the Appian
Way for a space of two miles with magnificent tombs, or have conceived and
executed the vastness of Caracalla's baths, or covered the Palatine Hill with
those splendid palaces which, through the liberality of the French emperor,

are now revealing their enormous substructions to the gaze of a fiftieth generation. These remains are unequalled, and will probably continue to be so till the end of time. They cannot fail to strike even the most phlegmatic spectator with astonishment and admiration; but beyond these feelings they awaken no thoughts on which the mind much loves to dwell. They speak of military rule and despotic power, of oppression abroad and tyranny at home. They are the tombs and may be regarded as the monuments of centuries of Roman liberty and prowess, and nothing less could have achieved or deserved them. But of the commonwealth itself, the true parent of these remains, the actual monuments are mean and few, and of the private life of the Romans there is not a trace.

An excursion to Pompeii, besides being the most interesting, is perhaps also one of the pleasantest that can be made from Naples. There is no burrowing under ground, no groping by torchlight as at Herculaneum, amidst damp and mouldy ruins some eighty or a hundred feet below the surface of the soil. On the contrary, Pompeii, as we have intimated, lies on a hill, exposed to the full influence of that brilliant Italian sun, and the genial breezes wafted over the bay of Naples. At whichever gate you enter you must ascend considerably to reach the Forum, nearly the highest point of the city. The streets, if narrow, are regular and clean, forming in this respect an agreeable contrast to those of Naples. The traveller who visits it from that city—one of the noisiest in Europe, not so much from the sound of carriage-wheels as of human lungs—will also be struck by the quiet that pervades Pompeii, as might naturally be expected in a city of the dead. The silence that reigns throughout, except when occasionally broken by a noisy party, is in excellent keeping with the scene, and allows free scope for those thoughts which cannot but enter the minds of the most unreflecting on visiting such a place.

However dreadful the eruption, it does not appear to have been so sudden in its effects but that most of the inhabitants of Pompeii might have made their escape had they possessed the requisite energy and resolution, or had been duly aware of the certainty of the fate that must overtake those who lingered behind. This is a legitimate inference from the fact that, although the amphitheatre was filled with spectators at the time of the catastrophe, only two or three skeletons have been found in it, and these probably belonged to gladiators who had been already killed or wounded. The greater part of the inhabitants must have taken to the sea or the road,

and probably succeeded in escaping the fiery shower; at all events, it is
certain that, regard being had to the size and importance of the place,
comparatively few bodies have been discovered.   But in a populous city like
Pompeii there must of course have been many lingerers; and though no
accurate computation has been made of the number of bodies found, it may
be safely reckoned at six hundred.   About forty skeletons have been discovered in the last four years, of course in a comparatively small part of the
excavated area; and, as not much more than a third part of the city has
been uncovered, an estimate in the same ratio would give a total loss of
about eighteen hundred lives.   As the population of Pompeii, on the lowest
calculation, consisted of twenty thousand souls, and may perhaps have
reached double that number, the percentage is a probable one; and though
in this view the catastrophe is terrible enough, yet it is hardly greater than
the circumstances might have led us to expect.   The victims doubtless consisted of the timid and irresolute, who were afraid, and of the sick, the aged
and infirm, who were unable to fly.   Some may have lingered behind from
motives of avarice and a wish to save their property; a few perhaps from
feelings of affection, and an unwillingness to abandon those whom they loved.
It might not perhaps be difficult to find illustrations of most of these causes
in the circumstances under which several of the bodies were discovered.

The sudden and appalling nature of the volcanic storm which burst over
the doomed city might have shaken the strongest nerves; while on those not
very firmly braced the effect must have been almost paralyzing.   Among the
weak and timid a first and natural impulse would have been to take shelter
in a lower room or cellar where the fiery shower could not penetrate, and
there abide till it had expended its fury.   This calculation, however, was
defeated by the duration of the eruption and by a change in its nature; the
lapillo being followed by showers of mud, which penetrated into crannies
where the ashes had not been able to enter.   And even without this muddy
deluge those who had betaken themselves to the lower apartments would in
most cases have eventually perished either from suffocation occasioned by
the mephitic vapours or from starvation, owing to their inability to force
their way out of the accumulated mass which had overwhelmed their place
of refuge.   A striking instance of such a case is recorded in the journals of
the superintendents of the excavations (Aug. 30th, 1787).   In the corridor
of a basement story were found the skeletons of a man and a dog.   The
human bones, however, did not hang together, but were strewed about the

place, and appeared to have been gnawed at the joints, while the skeleton of the dog was perfect. Only one inference can be drawn from this state of things. The man had evidently died first of hunger, while the dog had sustained life a little longer by feeding on his body.

The fatal effects of the showers of mud are strikingly illustrated by the well-known story connected with Diomed's suburban villa. Eighteen persons, mostly women, had taken shelter in the spacious quadrangular cellar which surrounds the garden, and were there overwhelmed by the entry of this liquid matter. Being of a slimy and tenacious nature, and hardening into a solid concrete, like plaster of Paris, the mud formed perfect moulds of the unfortunate persons whom it enveloped. The journals give so particular a description of this discovery that we shall here subjoin a translation. (Dec. 12th, 1772).

" It is plain that these eighteen persons, and perhaps others who may be discovered in the progress of the excavation, were surprised in this part of the house, where they had taken refuge, as best calculated to save them from destruction. But it availed not to protect them from a shower of ashes which fell after the *lapillo*, and was evidently accompanied with water, which served to introduce it into places where the first shower could not penetrate. This deluge of fluid matter, which after a time became a very tenacious earth, surrounded and enclosed all the substances which it met, and has preserved the impress and mould of them; as, for instance, of a wooden chest, and of a pile of small logs of wood. The same thing happened to the unfortunate human beings who have been discovered; of their flesh nothing has remained but the impress and mould of it in the earth, and within are the bones in their regular order. Even the hair on the skulls is partly preserved, and in some cases is seen to have been curled. Of the dresses nothing but the mere ashes have been found; but these ashes preserved traces of the quality of the materials, so that it could be easily seen whether the texture was coarse or fine. By way of proof of what is here said to have been observed, I caused as many as sixteen of these moulds of bodies to be cut open, in one of which is seen the bust of a female covered with a vest; while in all of these are remains of garments, and sometimes of two or three, one over the other. I also caused a head with hair on it to be carefully removed, and sent all these objects to the museum. From the little that I could distinguish of the vestments, it appeared that several of the persons had upon their heads cloths which descended to the shoulders:

that two or three dresses were worn over one another; that the stockings were of cloth and linen cut like long drawers; and that some had no shoes at all. The shoes observed seemed to belong to low servants or slaves. That one woman was superior to the rest could be perceived by the ornaments which she wore, by the fine texture of her dress, and by the coins which were found near her."

It is much to be regretted that the idea did not occur to this superintendent of taking a mould of these bodies, thus rendering their very forms in the last agonies of their death-struggle, as the Commendatore Fiorelli has done with such signal success with bodies found near a century afterwards. So slow a birth of time is sometimes even so simple an idea! The casts of the four bodies now exhibited in the street of Herculaneum are among the most impressive sights at Pompeii. There manhood in its full strength, and womanhood in its maturity and its early bloom, may be seen sinking alike under that fatal visitation. Nor has the spectacle anything of that repulsive kind which perhaps might strike us if we saw the bodies themselves. We gaze upon them as if they were so many pieces of statuary cast in Nature's own mould, much as we do upon the Dying Gladiator in the Capitol, and pronounce it one of the finest statues in the world.

If the members of Diomed's family discovered in the cellar perished from not adopting a sufficiently resolute course, Diomed himself, it has been thought, died from another of the causes which we have assigned—that of avarice. Instead of staying by his family he had preferred to fly; but, intent upon collecting his treasures, had apparently delayed his flight too long. His skeleton was found close to the garden gate, the key of which he held in his hand. On his finger was a serpent ring. The skeleton of a slave lay near him, who was carrying off a great number of various coins in a cloth. These men were probably killed by the mephitic vapours. "The ruling passion strong in death" is further illustrated at Pompeii by the many skeletons found of persons flying with what property they hoped to save. Many female skeletons especially have been discovered with all their "womans' world," their *mundus muliebris*, as the Latins called it, about them, their jewels, trinkets, and amulets.

They who perished from mere inability to fly cannot of course be recognized by any particular mark or circumstance, unless it be such as were evidently incarcerated. Nor can we distinguish those who lingered from affection, though there is one instance which might evidently bear such an interpretation. In a shop under the Old Baths were found the skeletons of a young man and a young woman locked together in a close embrace. Their age was shown by their fine and well-preserved teeth.

Besides swallowing up several important towns, the eruption of 79 disfigured the face of nature for miles around, rendered barren those fertile fields, and converted that smiling landscape into a mass of hideous ruins.

> Here verdant vines o'erspread Vesuvius' sides,
> The generous grape here pour'd her purple tides.
> This Bacchus loved beyond his native scene,
> Here dancing satyrs joy'd to trip the green.
> Far more than Sparta this in Venus' grace ;
> And great Alcides once renown'd the place :
> Now flaming embers spread dire waste around,
> And gods regret that gods can thus confound.
>
> MARTIAL. *Epig.* iv. 44.

The Emperor Titus formed the project of rebuilding Pompeii; but it came to nothing, either through his death, which ensued a year or two afterwards, or because it was discovered that the expense would exceed any probable returns, and that it was better to abandon a territory which, for many ages to come, seemed devoted to sterility. From the marks of having been opened and rifled, which may be observed in several of the houses, as well as from the fact that no very considerable sums of money have been found, it is plain that some of the inhabitants must have returned, and by means of excavations, recovered some of their most valuable property. Even down to the reign of Alexander Severus the place seems to have served as a sort of quarry; for that emperor is said to have procured from the buried city a great quantity of marble, columns and statues, for the purpose of embellishing the works which he erected at Rome. This circumstance may serve to account for the dilapidated appearance of many of the monuments; for it can hardly be supposed that they were reduced to that condition solely by the earthquake of the year 63.

In process of time Pompeii and its sisters in misfortune became entirely forgotten, and through a long night of ages seemed to sleep the sleep of death. The site on which it stood, and even its very name, sank into oblivion; although here and there the summit of some of its buildings cropped up above the soil, and the name of *civita*, or the city, which still lingered in the mouths of the peasants, might have served to indicate its position. After the revival of learning, indeed, the names of the buried cities sometimes

D

appear in Italian authors.   Nicolò Perotto mentions Pompeii, Herculaneum,
and Stabiæ in his "Cornucopia," published in 1488; the "Herculaneum
Oppidum" is indicated in the map of Ambrogio Leone, 1513, as the site
occupied by Portici : Leandro Alberti, in his "Descrizione di tutta l'Italia"
(1561), recalls the burying of Herculaneum, Pompeii, and Stabiæ by the
eruption of Vesuvius, and indicates the spots where they were then believed
to have existed.   A chapter in the "Historia Neapolitana" of Giulio Cesare
Capaccio, published in 1607, is devoted to the antiquities of Herculaneum.
Camillo Peregrino, in speaking of the same city in his "Apparato alle anti-
chità di Capua" (1651), thinks that it occupied the site of the present *Torre
del Greco;* and the same idea is adopted by Francesco Baldano in his work
entitled "L'antico Ercolano ovvero la Torre del Greco tolta dall' oblio,"
published in 1688.*   Nay, the celebrated architect, Dominico Fontana, being
employed in the year 1592 in constructing the subterranean canal, which
still exists, for conveying the waters of the Sarno to Torre del Greco,
actually conducted it under the site of Pompeii, and often found his work
obstructed by the foundations of the buildings; yet no curiosity was excited
to explore the vast remains which evidently existed there.

It is singular enough that, while so many palpable indications existed of
the remains of Pompeii, Herculaneum, a city buried to a depth of eighty or
a hundred feet, under a hard mass of lava and other accumulations of
volcanic matter, the deposits of many eruptions of Vesuvius, should have
been the first to be discovered, and that by a mere accident.

In 1684, a baker residing at Portici sunk a well on his premises, which,
after penetrating through some ancient ruins, terminated, at a depth of ninety
feet, near the stage of the theatre of Herculaneum.   A few years after,
Prince Emmanuel d'Elbœuf, of the house of Lorraine, having been sent to
Naples at the head of an imperial army, espoused there a daughter of the
Prince of Salsa, and purchased the ground containing the well, in order to
erect a palace.   About the year 1713, having occasion to enlarge the well,
he found some marbles, with which he adorned his stair-cases and terraces,
as well as some female statues; the latter, however, were claimed by the
imperial government, and the prince was compelled to send them to Vienna.
They are now in the palace of the King of Saxony, at Dresden.   In the
process of further excavations, the duke is said to have discovered a round
temple having forty-eight alabaster columns.   But for some reason or another

* See Breton, "Pompeia," p. 20.

the excavations were suspended till 1736, when they were resumed by order of King Charles III. A new entry was now effected at Resina, when the theatre, a basilica, and some private houses were discovered; but it was some years before it was ascertained, by means of coins and inscriptions, that these remains belonged to the ancient city of Herculaneum.

These discoveries had the effect of stimulating research, and led to the disinterment of Pompeii. Don Rocco Alcubierre, a Spanish colonel of engineers, who had been employed by Charles III. in the excavations at Herculaneum, was engaged in 1748 in examining Fontana's subterranean aqueduct or canal, which, as we have before said, passes underneath Pompeii, when he was informed by some inhabitants of Torre Annunziata, that certain ancient statues and other objects, as well as the ruins of a house, had been discovered about two miles from that place. The discoveries at Herculaneum led him to conclude that some ancient city lay buried there, and having obtained permission to search the place, he commenced his excavations at the spot now called the Street of Fortune. His labours were speedily rewarded by the discovery of a large fresco painting, and soon afterwards the skeleton of a man, with several pieces of coin lying near him, was found on the surface of the *lapillo* or ashes, covered with the hardened mud. The researches were now pushed on with some vigour, and before the end of 1748 the amphitheatre was excavated. A regular journal of the discoveries began now to be kept, at first in the Spanish language, and after 1764 in Italian. It is remarkable that in this journal the amphitheatre is styled the amphitheatre of Stabiæ. To that town, which is now known to have occupied the site of Castellamare, the remains discovered were for several years attributed, and it is not till 1756 that we find the name of Pompeii mentioned in the journals. It does not appear what caused this name to be inserted; but any doubts that might have been entertained respecting the identity of the city must have been satisfactorily removed by the discovery, in 1763, of an inscription in the Street of the Tombs, recording that the Emperor Vespasian had restored to the municipality of Pompeii all public ground diverted by private persons to their own use.

Such were the causes which accidentally led to the disinterment of Pompeii, and conferred upon it a celebrity much greater than that which it had enjoyed in antiquity. There are some cities, as well as some men, that owe their renown to their misfortunes; and, but for some signal and over-whelming calamity, would never have been heard of by posterity. Such

was the case with Pompeii and its neighbour cities. Third rate towns,
without a history of their own, cast entirely into the shade by the brilliant
fortunes of the capital, and lost, like mere specks, in the vast extent of the
Roman empire, even their names would scarcely have survived in the
wreck of ages, had not the sudden eruption of an unsuspected volcano
embalmed them for immortality. Thrown open for our inspection almost
in the very manner in which they existed in antiquity, they have enabled
us to realize an idea of ancient Roman life which it would have been impossible to acquire from the descriptions of books; and, apart from considera-
tions of art, present to the educated and inquiring traveller more numerous
and more striking objects of interest than can be found even in the Roman
capital itself.

  After the first impulse, the excavations at Pompeii proceeded but slowly,
and were conducted in anything but a proper spirit. Instead of being
prosecuted out of love for classical antiquity, and a desire to extend the
knowledge of it, the main purposes of the directors of them seemed to be to
discover articles of marketable value, or such objects of art as might serve
to adorn the royal collections. Winkelmann, in his letters describing the
discoveries at Herculaneum, records an anecdote which illustrates the spirit
to which we have alluded. On the summit of the theatre at that place was
a quadriga, with a figure in the car of the size of life; the whole was of gilt
bronze, placed on a basis of white marble, which may still be seen. Some
persons indeed say that instead of one car with four horses, there were three
cars having two horses each; a variation which only serves to show the utter
carelessness and want of intelligence of those who conducted the excavations.
These sculptures, as may be readily imagined, had been overthrown and
mutilated by the eruption; nevertheless, at the time of their discovery all
the fragments were in existence. Now, how were these invaluable remains
treated? They were thrown pell-mell into a cart, carried to Naples, dis-
charged in a court of the castle, and thrown in a heap into a corner! Here
they remained a long while, being looked upon as no better than old iron;
till, at last, it having been perceived that several of the pieces had been
purloined, it was resolved to apply the remainder to some honourable use.
And what might we suppose this to be? A great part of the metal was
melted to form two large busts of the King and Queen! Out of the fragments that remained, however, by dint of patience and talent, one of the
horses was reconstructed. It now forms one of the most admirable objects

in the museum at Naples; but at the same time awakens melancholy reflections on this act of royal vandalism.

The same plan was followed at Pompeii. The chief objects of search were statues, paintings, jewellery, and articles in gold and silver, which were destined to enrich the royal collections. No care was taken to preserve the houses in which they were found; on the contrary, these were often again filled up with the rubbish of an adjoining excavation; nor were any plans made of the streets and houses that had been uncovered. The works were conducted in secrecy and mystery, and it was with the greatest difficulty that any stranger could obtain admission to them. The visitors were chiefly royal, noble, or otherwise distinguished persons, who had interest enough to obtain the *entrée;* and from these some of the houses have derived their names, from having been excavated in their presence. We should rather say, however, the final excavation, technically called a *scavo;* when the last few feet of ashes, amongst which articles of value or curiosity are commonly found, were removed. It may be readily imagined that great personages were not invited on these occasions unless some interesting discoveries were likely to be made; and it has even been suspected that means were sometimes taken to prevent such visits from ending in disappointment.

Among these royal visits, the journals of the excavations record one made by the eccentric and energetic Emperor Joseph II. on the 7th of April, 1769, in company with his empress, his minister Count Kaunitz. the King and Queen of Naples, Sir W. Hamilton, the English ambassador, and some distinguished antiquaries. The *find* on this occasion was particularly good. So many were the articles turned up that Joseph hinted his suspicions to Signor La Vega, the superintendent. that they had been purposely placed there " to flatter his good fortune:" but the superintendent assured him that such was not the case, and in support of his assertion pointed to the situation of the articles, and the nature of the soil. A subsequent observation of La Vega's to his royal master, "that such a pleasure had been reserved for him alone among all sovereigns," renders, however, his good faith on this occasion somewhat doubtful. La Vega having informed the Emperor that only thirty persons were employed on the works, he asked the King of Naples how he could suffer so great a work to proceed so languidly? The king replied, in true Italian style, that by degrees—*a poco a poco*—all would be accomplished; when Joseph rejoined that so great a work required three thousand men, that there was nothing like it in Europe. Asia, Africa.

or America, and that it was an especial honour to the kingdom of Naples. If, after the lapse of near a century, Joseph could return to life and pay another visit to Pompeii, he would still find the excavations proceeding with not much greater rapidity, though perhaps he might be surprised to find how many fine things the *a poco a poco* system of his Neapolitan majesty had succeeded in bringing to light. At the present rate of proceeding, the whole city may, perhaps, be uncovered in two more centuries; that is, if Vesuvius can be persuaded to forbear from again swallowing it up. A company formed for its disinterment, by way of a commercial speculation, might perform the whole task in less than ten years. As it is, we must console ourselves with the reflection that the present mode of proceeding will excite and gratify the curiosity of our children's children to the fifth or sixth generation.

The house visited by Joseph II. on this occasion, situated at the side of the Triangular Forum, was named after him. It was a fine house; but little or nothing can be seen there now, as, according to the barbarous system formerly followed, it was again filled up. Other houses have also derived their names from the visits of royal and distinguished personages, as those of Francis II, of the Grand Duke of Tuscany, of the Emperor of Russia, of the King of Prussia, of the Russian Princes, of the Queen of England—Adelaide, who visited Pompeii in 1838. Perhaps the best deserved of these titles *in honorem* is that of the houses of Championnet, near the Forum, since they were excavated under the directions of the French general of that name, at the end of the last century. Other houses have been called after pictures, statues, mosaics, or other objects found in them, or from the presumed profession of their owners: as the House of the Anchor, of the Faun, of the Hunt, of the great and little Fountains, of the Figured Capitals, of the Black Walls, of the Surgeon, of the Tragic Poet, &c. In a few cases they have been named after the presumed owners, as the House of Diomed, of Cicero, of Pansa, of Sallust, &c. But the only houses of which the owners' names have been discovered with any certainty, are those of M. Lucretius and Cornelius Rufus. In the former, in a small cabinet or study, was a painting representing a waxed tablet, a style, and other writing materials, together with a folded letter, on which was the address, "To M. Lucretius, Flamen of Mars, and Decurion of Pompeii." The proprietor of the other house, Cornelius Rufus, has succeeded in transmitting not only his name, but also his portrait, to posterity, by setting up in one corner of his hall, or atrium, a well-executed marble bust of himself, of the size of life, with his name inscribed underneath. It will be seen in the photograph of the House of Rufus given further on. These two Pompeian magnates probably little dreamed that they should secure for themselves so lasting a remembrance by these contrivances.

During the reign of the Bourbon dynasty at Naples, the excavations at Pompeii went on much in the fashion just described. The period of the French occupation of Naples (1806-1815), was marked by a more vigorous prosecution of the researches; and it was during this period that the Forum, the greater part of the Street of the Tombs, and the line of the walls were laid open. Murat's wife, Queen Caroline, took great interest in the excavations, and it was under her patronage that Mazois commenced his magnificent work on Pompeii. After the restoration of the Bourbons, the works again proceeded slowly; though, even at this snail's pace, much of course was done in the period of nearly half a century, during which they occupied the throne. The most important excavations conducted during this period were those of several temples round the Forum, of the public Baths, and of many large and interesting houses, as those of the Tragic Poet, of the Faun, of the Fountain, the Fullonica, and others. The revolution, which drove the Bourbons from the throne, had ultimately the effect of also revolutionizing the proceedings at Pompeii; though not so much in increasing the speed of the operations, as in causing them to be more carefully conducted. Garibaldi, who became dictator at Naples in 1859, made indeed a lamentable choice in appointing the romance writer, M. Alexandre Dumas, to the directorship of the excavations. That gentleman, however brilliant his talents, seems to have been totally unfit for the post, and is said scarcely to have visited Pompeii. His tenure of office, however, was fortunately short. When the authority of Victor Emmanuel, as King of Italy, became established in the Neapolitan dominions, the superintendence of the excavations was intrusted to the Commendatore Fiorelli, who still continues to hold it. This gentleman had long been known as a scholar and antiquary, and as in every respect excellently qualified for the office; his liberal political opinions had, however, not only excluded him from it, but even drawn down upon him the persecution of the government. The peculiar excellence of Signor Fiorelli's system consists in the skilful mode in which the excavations are conducted, the religious care with which every fragment is retained in or restored to its original position, and the pains taken to preserve the frescoes and other

ornaments from being damaged by the atmosphere.   To this system we owe
the restoration, the only instance of it, of the second story of one of the
houses, together with its projecting *mænianum*, or balcony.   The house in
question, which, from the characteristic feature just mentioned, has been
called the *Casa del Balcone Pensile*, or House of the Hanging Balcony, a name
which it has also given to the lane in which it stands, is small and mean,
and possesses little else to attract attention, except perhaps a pretty fountain
in its court—for it cannot be called an atrium.   We have annexed a photograph of it.

We are also indebted to Signor Fiorelli's ingenuity for the plaster casts
of the bodies to which we have already alluded.

Such, then, is the history, in brief, of the origin of Pompeii, of its ancient
existence, of the terrible calamity by which it was overwhelmed, of its rediscovery, and of the process of its disinterment.   We shall now proceed to
give some account of its general appearance, of its public and private buildings, and generally of those objects which are most likely to attract the
attention of the visitor.

Pompeii, as we have said, is situated on a hill, or plateau, of an oval or
egg-like form, and of moderate elevation; so that on whatever side we enter,
there is a gentle ascent to the highest point of the city, which lies about the
Forum.   The greatest diameter is but little more than three quarters of a
mile, while the breadth is under half a mile, and the whole circuit of the
walls not quite two miles.   Of the space thus enclosed, considerably more
than a third has been excavated on the western side of the town.   The walls
run round the whole town, except on the western side, where the declivity
is so steep, forming almost a cliff, as to render needless any artificial defence.
Some writers have supposed that in ancient times this side of the town was
washed by the sea, and that the tract of land, about a mile in extent, which
now intervenes between the town and the shore, was formed by the deposits
of the great eruption.   But this, for many reasons, does not seem probable;
and Overbeck, one of the most recent inquirers into this subject, informs us,
in his work on Pompeii, that he has discovered traces of ancient buildings
and other remains on the ground said to have been formerly covered by
the sea.

The walls consist, in their lower parts, of large blocks of hewn, but not
squared, stone, fitted together without mortar; the joinings of them presenting to the eye a vast variety of angles.   The upper part of the wall is of a

24ª

FOUNTAIN IN HOUSE OF THE BALCONY.

more regular and improved construction, and therefore probably of a later date: the stones being more regularly cut, and approaching that style of masonry which the Greeks call *isodomon;* that is, constructed of stones of the same form and size. Some parts, however, are even more recent than this, consisting of what is called *opus incertum;* or of small pieces of stone or lava, cemented together with mortar, and coated over with stucco, in imitation of the ancient parts. These portions are supposed to have been repairs to make good the damage inflicted by Sulla.

The wall was in fact a double one, the two being bonded together by cross walls between them, and the interstices filled up with earth, so as to form a broad agger, or mound, about twenty feet thick. Both the external and the internal wall were capped with battlements to defend the soldiers who guarded them, and were provided with embrasures through which they might hurl their missiles. The external wall, which inclines slightly inwards, was about twenty-five feet in height, and was unprotected by a ditch. The inner wall, which was a few feet higher, could have been of no service against an external enemy, and seems to have been designed only to give a more imposing appearance to the defences. At intervals, square towers rose from the walls, which in some parts, as near the Gate of Herculaneum, are at the distance of about eighty paces from one another; while in other places they are two or three hundred, and sometimes nearly five hundred paces apart. They consist of several stories. Each had a sally port and an archway, through which the troops might pass along the wall. About ten of these towers may still be counted. They are evidently of more recent date than the walls, though in a very ruinous state. It is hardly probable that their condition is the effect of the earthquakes which preceded and accompanied the eruption of the year 79; and it has, therefore, been sometimes not improbably conjectured that their dilapidated state, which is chiefly observable on their outer face, was the effect of Sulla's siege at the end of the Social War.

Pompeii appears to have had eight gates. The principal one, the Gate of Herculaneum, so called from its spanning the Via Domitiana, a branch of the Appian Way, which led from Herculaneum, and consequently from Rome and northern Italy, stood at the north-western extremity of the town. We shall have occasion to describe this gate further on. Hence, proceeding round the walls in an easterly direction, the other gates occur in the following order: the Gate of Vesuvius, the Gate of Capua, the Gate of Nola, the

E

Gate of the Sarnus, the Gate of Stabiæ, the Gate of the Theatres, and the Sea Gate, or Porta della Marina. The gate which we have here called the Gate of Stabiæ has been sometimes named the Gate of Nocera, and the former name given to the Gate of the Theatres; an arrangement which is more in accordance with the name of Strada Stabiana, given to the street which issues out at the gate next the theatres. Between the Gate of the Theatres, or of Stabiæ, and the Gate of Herculaneum, a space that includes half the southern and all the western side of the city, the walls can no longer be traced, but in this portion of the circumference there was probably one or two more gates. The Porta della Marina, the only one now between the two, is a long vaulted passage of steep ascent; and, from its being near the railway station, forms the most frequented entrance to Pompeii. The ground between this gate and that of Herculaneum is, as we have before said, abrupt and cliff-like, and was probably never defended by a wall; at all events, its place is now occupied by tall houses of several stories, the upper parts of which may be entered from the street leading from the Gate of Herculaneum.

Of the gates just enumerated only that of Nola and that of the Theatres are interesting from their antiquity, being evidently much older than the Roman occupation. The construction of the Gate of Nola is particularly remarkable. It does not, like the other gates, begin at the outer line of the wall, but like the Gate of the Lions at Mycenæ, at the end of a passage formed of strong masonry, and not much broader than the gateway, which penetrates into the city beyond the inner wall. This mode of construction afforded an advantage to the garrison by enabling them to ply assailants with darts, arrows, stones, and other missiles as they thronged up the narrow passage. When viewed from within, the gate appears to have been partly built of blocks of hewn stone and partly of brick, the latter portion being doubtless of a later date. On the keystone of the arch is sculptured a head in high relief, as was customary among the Etruscans—an object which likewise serves to show the high antiquity of this gate. There is at the side of it an inscription in the Oscan tongue, the wrong interpretation of which caused this gate to be called for a long time the "Gate of Isis;" but scholars have now discovered that the inscription has no reference to that goddess, the words only meaning that Vibius Popidius, the Medixtuticus, or chief magistrate of Pompeii, had caused the gate to be erected, and had approved of it when completed.

STREET OF THE TOMBS.

The Gate of Stabiæ, or that near the theatres, first discovered in 1851, appears also to be very ancient. The walls near it are of a very antique style of masonry, consisting of huge blocks of stone put together without mortar. The holes for bolts show that this gate was not closed like that of Herculaneum, with a portcullis, but with strong double doors. An Oscan inscription was also found in this gateway mentioning the names of some streets and other objects in Pompeii.

Of all these gates only three are now used for the purpose of entering the city—namely, the Sea Gate, the Herculaneum Gate, and the Gate of Stabiæ. The last, however, being on the south side of the city, and consequently out of the way of visitors from Naples, is seldom used. Whether the visitor should enter by the Sea Gate, or that of Herculaneum, is a matter that must be referred entirely to taste and convenience. The Sea Gate is more handy for those who travel by the railroad, and leads more directly to the Forum and the principal parts of the city. The Herculaneum gate is equally, or perhaps more convenient for visitors in carriages, and conveys a better idea of the approach to an ancient Roman town. The road which leads to it, called *Strada delle Tombe*, is lined on both sides with tombs, as shown in the annexed photograph. These tombs, from their comparative magnificence, may be supposed to have belonged to the leading families of Pompeii; and in this way, to compare small things with great, the traveller may be reminded of the approach to Rome by the Appian Way. As at the capital, the other entrances to Pompeii present but few tombs. The remains of a burial-place outside the Gate of Nola are supposed to have belonged to Alexandrians, who formed part of the population. It is well known that the burying or burning of a dead body within the precincts of a city was forbidden by the decemviral laws—a piece of civilization which, in spite of our superior refinement, we have only just begun to imitate. Driven thus beyond the walls, the rich and great seem to have preferred the most travelled roads for the last resting-place of their ashes; and as the Via Appia was the queen of ways, so also the Via Domitiana, which was a branch of it, formed the principal approach to Pompeii.

Before entering the town we will linger awhile among the objects presented in the view.

The first building on the right, having an open doorway, entered by three steps from the street, and having a gable over it, is the *Triclinium Funebre*, or dining room, in which, after the last honours had been rendered to the dead, a feast called *silicernium* was given by the relatives. This was a usual tribute of respect, but it was not an indispensable ceremony, and a disappointed heir would sometimes avenge himself by defrauding the deceased of this part of his funeral honours. An inscription in the gable informs us that it was erected in honour of Cn. Vibrius Saturninus, by his *libertus*, or freedman, Callistus. On entering, the visitor finds himself in a small quadrangular space surrounded with walls, but without a roof. At the top are the three stone benches forming the triclinium, with a square table between; before which stands the round basis of an altar for offerings. Originally the walls were richly painted, being divided into square panels or compartments by borders; each panel having in its centre a representation of some bird or animal: but these paintings have now almost entirely disappeared.

VIEW OF THE FUNERAL TRICLINIUM.

Next to the Triclinium is seen the tomb of Nævoleia Tyche, surrounded with a wall, entered by a door from the street. It is among the handsomest at Pompeii. Within the enclosure is a sepulchral chamber, surmounted by a marble monument in the form of an altar, placed on a basis or podium, with two steps.

On the front of this altar is a portrait of the foundress in bas-relief, with an inscription purporting that Nævoleia Tyche, the freedwoman of Lucius Nævoleius, had erected this mausoleum during her lifetime for herself and for L. Munatius Faustus, Augustal, and Paganus (or member of the suburban Council of the Pagus, Augustus Felix); to whom the Decurions, with the consent of the people, had granted the honour of the Bisellium (a chair of state) for his deserts: also for her and his freedmen and women. Under the inscription is another bas-relief with many figures, supposed to represent an offering to the dead, or the dedication of the tomb. The whole is surrounded with a rich and elegant arabesque border. There were found in the sepulchre several funeral urns for the ashes of the dead, mostly of terra cotta; but three were of glass, preserved in leaden cases of the same shape. One of them was of a large size. They are said to have contained

BAS-RELIEF ON THE MONUMENT OF NÆVOLEIA TYCHE.

burnt bones, swimming in a liquid composed of water, wine, and oil,—the last libations probably of friends.

On the side of the monument next the Triclinium is a ship sculptured in bas-relief, as may be seen in our photographic view. The prow is surmounted by a bust of Minerva; the poop terminates in a swan's neck, over which floats a flag; while another flag is to be seen at the mast head. The crew mostly consists of children, who are climbing the ropes and furling the sail. A man sitting at the rudder is supposed to represent Munatius, and the whole design to indicate that he was a sailor by profession; while others have imagined that it is allegorical, and symbolizes arrival in the haven of eternity after the stormy voyage of life.

BAS-RELIEF ON THE TOMB OF NÆVOLEIA TYCHE.

On the side opposite to the ship is sculptured the bisellium mentioned in the inscription. The seat, as its name implies, is capacious enough to hold two persons; but a single square footstool placed beneath the middle of it indicates that it is reserved for one.

The next place of burial, which is merely a square enclosure without any monument, belonged, as we learn from an inscription on the wall, to the family of Istacidius, and that it was fifteen feet long by fifteen deep. This last piece of intelligence has been used to determine the relative length of the Roman foot. The area contains two or three funereal cippi, low square columns, surmounted by a hemisphere said to be peculiar to Pompeii. These were sometimes adorned at the back with long tresses carved in resemblance of human hair, which awaken unclassical reminiscences of a barber's block.

Next is the cenotaph of the Augustal, C. Calventius Quietus, a monument which for purity of taste may rank among the best in the street. In a court of about twenty-one feet square rises a square massive basement of masonry five and a-half feet high, originally covered with stucco, on which is placed a square altar-shaped monument of marble, somewhat resembling that of Nævoleia Tyche, and approached from the base by three steps. On the front face, which is surrounded with a rich border, is an inscription recording that by a decree of the Decurions (the senate or court of aldermen of Pompeii), and with the consent of the people, the honour of the *bisellium* had been granted to Calventius Quietus, as a reward for his munificence. On the sides of the monument are garlands of oak-leaves bound with fillets. There is no door of entry to this tomb, for being a mere cenotaph it would not have to be opened to receive bodies; but the wall towards the street, being hardly four feet high, allows the passengers to inspect the monument. The side walls are much higher, while that at the back rises into a pediment. At the corners of the wall are square pinnacles, called *acroteria*, the sides of which were adorned with reliefs and stucco, now almost obliterated. One of these represented Theseus in the Labyrinth reposing after his labours; another, Œdipus and the Sphinx. The Theban hero, by putting his finger to his forehead, shows that he has in his head the solution of the riddle. One of these sculptures represented a young woman with a torch in her hand, and, according to Overbeck, another on her shoulder. She is supposed to be performing the funeral ceremony of kindling the pile, which was done, with averted face, by the nearest relative.

Adjoining the cenotaph is an empty walled area, on which it is conjectured a tomb was intended to be erected. This is followed by a large family sepulchre; but, as there is no inscription on it, the name of the owner is unknown. It consists of a short round tower on a quadrangular basis. The sepulchral chamber had a sort of bell-shaped vaulting, which often occurs in Turkish architecture, but of which, according to Overbeck, there is no other ancient instance. The walls which surround the tower and enclose the burying-place are surmounted at intervals with square pinnacles or *acroteria*, resembling those in the sepulchre of Calventius Quietus. These were in like manner ornamented with bas-reliefs in stucco. One of the most striking of these represents a young woman in the act of depositing a funereal fillet on the skeleton of a child, which reposes on a heap of stones.

Next in order is the monument commonly called the Tomb of Scaurus; a name, however, which, according to Millin, Mommsen, and Overbeck, rests on no certain foundation. It consists of a square chamber serving as a basement, and surmounted by three steps, on which is a massive square *cippus* of brick. The front face of this *cippus* has a marble slab with a mutilated inscription. The chief interest of this monument, which is not remarkable for beauty or taste, consists in the bas-reliefs with which the upper part of the sepulchral chamber and the steps of the *cippus* are covered, but which at present can only be partially made out. They represented gladiatorial combats and *venationes*, or fights with wild beasts; and, as they were fortunately copied when in a good state of preservation, they have been of much service in illustrating those bloody sports.

Some way further on, just under one of the cypress-trees in the view, is the tomb of an unknown owner, a good deal resembling those of Nævoleia Tyche and Calventius Quietus, as it consists of a square altar-shaped monument or *cippus*, with two steps, and rests on a quadrangular basis of squared stone. It is commonly said, though without much apparent reason, that this sepulchre was only in process of construction at the time of the eruption. It possesses nothing of interest to detain us.

Beyond this the succession of the tombs on this side of the way is interrupted for a considerable space, and after passing an enclosed area adjoining the peristyle of the so-called Villa of Cicero, we come to a row of shops which may possibly have been the property of the owner of the villa. The openings of these shops are seen in the photographic view. Beyond them the perspective becomes too distant to discern objects clearly, except the Gate of Herculaneum, which stands at the top of the street. We shall here, however, briefly describe the objects which intervene between the shops and the gate. Beyond the shops a narrow lane turns up to the right, just before arriving at which is the entrance to Cicero's Villa. On the other side of the lane are three funereal monuments consisting of a tomb, now in ruins, between two large semicircular exedræ, or seats, made of stone, and uncovered. The first of these seats is about seventeen feet in diameter. On the wall above the bench is an inscription in large letters purporting that this burial-place was assigned by a decree of the Decurions to Mamia, a public priestess. The further seat very much resembles that already described. An inscription identifies it as belonging to Aulus Veius, a duumvir of justice and military tribune, to whom the ground had been presented by the Decurions and the people. It has been sometimes doubted whether the tomb between the two seats is that of Mamia, or another and handsomer one, which stands immediately behind the first seat. The latter, however, from inscriptions in it relating to various persons, seems not to have been a private place of burial, but a sepulchre common to many, and designed apparently to receive the ashes of priests. This tomb, which resembles a small temple, is of masonry covered with stucco, and ornamented with engaged columns, apparently Corinthian; but, as their capitals are gone, this is uncertain. At a spot behind this tomb many half-burnt bones of animals have been found; and as a richly ornamented altar was dug up here, we may perhaps conclude that it was used for sacrifices to the dead. Near here were also found graves covered with flat tiles and containing entire human skeletons, which must therefore have been interred without having been burnt.

The only other object to be noticed on this side of the street is a small square recess with a vaulted roof, which stands between the last semicircular seat and the gate of the town. From its position here it was long taken to be, and still is by some, a sentry-box; and a wonderful story has obtained great credit and circulation how the skeleton of a soldier was found in it, who, rather than desert his post, died at it, the victim of Roman discipline. But the truth is no such discovery was made, as may be seen by referring to the journals of the excavations, under date August 13th, 1763. The same entry records an inscription found in it, purporting that the place was given by the Decurions to the Augustal M. Cerrinius Restitutus; and it may therefore be regarded as his sepulchre.

We are now arrived at the Gate of Herculaneum, but we have not yet inspected the tombs on the other side of the way, and we must therefore retrace our steps before entering the town. The objects on the left-hand side of the street, however, are hardly so important as those on the right; and as, owing to the perspective, they are not seen so clearly in the view, we shall be brief in our description of them.

Close to the city gate, and nearly opposite to the supposed sentry-box, stands a pedestal for a colossal statue. Next to this, in descending the street, but divided from it by a narrow lane, stands the cenotaph of the ædile Titus Terentius Felix. This is followed by three or four unimportant tombs, which we need not stop to describe. We need only mention that in the smallest of them was found a vase of dark blue glass, now in the national museum, considered to be, after the celebrated Portland vase, the finest ancient specimen of this sort of art. From this discovery the tomb has obtained the name of *Tomba del Vaso di vetro blu*. The glass, which is transparent, is encircled with a white opaque relief representing cupids or geniuses gathering grapes and preparing the vintage amid rich foliage, while others are playing on the pipes or the lyre. At the lower part of the design are on either side of the vase two masks, one male, the other female, while a narrow border encircles the bottom of it, on which are represented animals feeding or reposing. A coloured plate of this vase will be found in Zahn's "Ornamente aller classischen Kunst-epochen," Haft xi.

Next to this tomb is a small semicircular niche with a stone bench running round it, similar to the *exedra* on the other side of the way already described; only this is covered in with a vaulted roof, with a pediment above, and has rich, though somewhat bizarre, architectural ornaments. Beyond this seat is a row of shops somewhat similar to those on the other side of the way. Before them projects an archway that spans the footpath, as will be seen in the view. Towards the end of this row of buildings, the road divides into two, leaving between the branches a sort of angular tongue, where the tombs begin again. One which stands in the middle of the road, just at the point were it diverges, built for the most part in *opus reticulatum*, is called the Tomb with the Marble Door, as no inscription acquaints us with the name of its owner. The marble door is about four feet high: it turned on brass pivots, and was fastened with a lock. It is kept closed, but the key may be obtained by application in the proper quarter. The interior consists of a vaulted chamber, lighted by a small window in the roof. A stone bench or ledge runs around it, on which, as well as in the vaulted niches under it, and in the side walls, were deposited urns or vases. This arrangement gives it the appearance of a small *columbarium*. There were also several bronze lamps, which may have served to illuminate the tomb at the festival of the *Feralia*, and other times when the Romans visited the ashes of their deceased parents and relatives, to make offerings to their manes, called *parentalia* and *inferiæ*. Opposite the entrance, in a square niche

F

with a gable, was a large alabaster vase containing ashes, supposed to be those of the proprietor of the tomb. In the road, immediately before this tomb, is a small enclosed space, which is thought to have been a private *ustrinum*, or place for burning dead bodies.

On the tongue of ground between the two roads several tombs lie close together. The first from that of the Marble Door is an unfinished sepulchre. Next to this, close to the trottoir, and nearly facing the burying ground of Nistacidius, which we have already described as lying between the tombs of Nævoleia Tyche and Calventius Quietus, stands the sepulchre of Libella. It is a solid structure, composed of blocks of travertine, and rises in the shape of an altar, or of the pedestal of a column, to a height of sixteen feet, the base being about twelve feet square. It has a moulding and cornice, which may be seen in the view. Beneath is an inscription purporting that the site of the monument was presented by the public to two of the Libella family; namely, to the father, M. Alleius Luccius Libella, who was an ædile, duumvir of justice, prefect, and quinquennial; and to his son, a decurion, who died at the age of seventeen: and that Alleia Decimilla, public priestess of Ceres, had erected on it the monument to her husband and son. Cicero, in one of his letters, replies to a friend who had solicited his interest in obtaining the post of decurion at Pompeii, that it was an easier thing to become a senator at Rome. We may, therefore, infer from the fact of the younger Libella having obtained that office at so early an age, that the family was one of considerable distinction. There is no sepulchral chamber within the monument, and it must therefore be regarded as a cenotaph, although it is not so characterized in the inscription; unless, indeed, there be a grave underneath.

Behind this tomb is a small quadrangular walled space, thought to have been a burial place for poorer citizens, or a private ustrinum. Further on is a group of four or five more tombs. These have nothing to arrest our attention; except the one which closes the line of tombs on this side, and appears from an inscription to have been the family vault of M. Arrius Diomedes. It stands just opposite to the entrance of the suburban villa; to which indeed it has given a name, though there is nothing, except its proximity, to connect it with the owner of the villa. It consists of a platform, or basis, of *opus incertum*, on which are several monuments. It is bounded on the left by a wall, near which stand two funereal cippi with hemispheres, of the kind already described; erected apparently in memory of a son and daughter of Arrius. These are divided by a low wall from the principal monument; but an inscription precisely under this wall shows that the whole group belonged to the same family. The chief tomb is a temple-like building, about nine feet broad and twelve high, with two pilasters at the sides supporting a pediment. A double door, with the fasces and hatchets sculptured on each, but reversed, as on occasions of mourning, indicate the magisterial dignity of the founder; which is further confirmed by an inscription over them, stating that the freedman, M. Arrius Diomedes, chief magistrate (*magister*) of the suburb of Augustus Felix had erected the monument in memory of himself and family.

From the last resting-place of Diomedes we will step over the street, and take a brief view of the reputed dwelling of his family. This suburban villa was discovered at a very early period of the excavations, but is still the most extensive of the private buildings at Pompeii. It is the only house in the place provided with a portico, which will be seen in the annexed cut. The

house is approached by a flight of lofty steps, for it was built at the side of a hill or ridge, and the ground falling away at the back, afforded opportunity to construct a spacious suite of rooms under the peristyle. We cannot, however, linger on the details of the building, which could not be understood without a ground-plan, and must content ourselves with describing its principal features. After passing through a small triangular vestibule, if it deserve that name, the visitor finds him-

PORTICO OF THE HOUSE OF DIOMEDES, WITH A VIEW OF THE ATRIUM BEYOND.

self in a handsome peristyle, which in country houses, according to the precept of Vitruvius, occupied the place of the atrium. At the time of the discovery, the columns, capitals, and entablatures, which were of an elegant order, were in a good state of preservation, as well as the paintings on the walls. The lower part of the columns, to the height of one third, are unfluted and painted red, while the upper part is white and fluted. The pavement is of *opus Siyninum*, a composition of pounded tile and mortar.

which derived its name from the town of Signia, the place probably where it was invented. In the middle of the peristyle was an *impluvium* surrounded with fourteen columns. The water received in the *piscina* fed a cistern below. The peristyle was surrounded with bed-rooms and other offices in the usual fashion. On the side of it next the street, to the left of the entrance, was a private bath on a large scale, with a small portico, and the usual suite of apartments and other appurtenances found in the public baths, such as an apodyterium, frigidarium, tepidarium, &c. On the opposite, or further side of the peristyle, in the place usually occupied by the tablinum in Roman houses, was a sort of large hall, with other adjoining apartments; behind which ran a long gallery with windows looking over two terraces towards the garden. Between these terraces was a large hall, or *œcus*, with a window reaching almost to the ground, and affording a splendid prospect over the Bay of Naples from Castellamare to Torre Annunziata, including in the distance the islands of Capri, Procida, and Ischia. The decorations of the apartments were elegant and in good taste; but no remarkable pictures or mosaics were discovered in them, though many articles of value were found. At the back of the villa was a garden upwards of one hundred feet square, surrounded with a crypto-porticus at a considerably lower level than the peristyle and gallery. Under the peristyle, as we have before said, were various apartments, destined apparently for servants and household purposes, but in so ruinous a state that it is impossible to guess at their destination. In them was found the skeleton of a man, and near it that of a goat, with a bell round its neck. In the middle of the garden was a large quadrangular basin with a jet-d'eau, and behind an enclosed space covered with a trellis. At each corner of the extremity of the garden were two small apartments, one perhaps an oratory. A cellar ran underneath three sides of the portico surrounding the garden, the floor of which was raised four steps above the level of the garden, in order to give the cellar the requisite height. A great many *amphoræ* showed that it was used as a wine cellar. It was near the entrance of it that the eighteen skeletons were found, which we have already described, besides the bodies at the garden gate, supposed to be those of the master and his slave. Altogether the remains of thirty-three persons were discovered in this house.

We must now retrace our steps up the Street of the Tombs, in order to enter Pompeii by the Gate of Herculaneum. In size and arrangement it bears some resemblance to Temple Bar, consisting of a central entrance for carriages, about fourteen feet and a-half wide, and two small side entrances for foot passengers, vaulted over; but the top has now fallen in, and the arch is imperfect. It was a double gate; the outer defence being a portcullis, whilst the inner one towards the town consisted of folding doors. There appears to have been a large aperture in the vaulting of the carriage entrance, by means of which assailants who had broken through the portcullis might be attacked with missiles while preparing to batter down the second doors. The gate is evidently one of the more recent ones, and a Roman work. Close to it, on the left in the inside, is a flight of high and narrow steps, by which the wall may be ascended. The alternate layers of brick and lava with which the gate is constructed were plastered over with a fine white stucco, which, at the time when it was excavated, was covered on the outside with a number of inscriptions; unfortunately, however, for the most part illegible. These inscriptions had been traced over previous ones which had been effaced by a fresh coating of white.

The Gate of Herculaneum must, from its situation, have formed, as we have already observed, the principal entrance to Pompeii. Yet the street in which we find ourselves after passing it, called the *Strada Consolare*, or Consular Street, is by no means one of the best in the town. It is narrow and somewhat crooked, and must have been surpassed in appearance by several others in the place, as the Street of Fortune, the Street of Mercury, the Street of the Forum, the Street of Abundance, &c. Yet there are some notable houses in passing up it; as, on the left hand side, the House of the Vestals—very inappropriately so called, to judge from some pictures found in it—the House of the Surgeon, deriving its name from some surgical instruments in it, which very much resemble those now in use, and show that there is little new under the sun; and a building that has been called the *Dogana*, or custom house, principally on the strength of some scales and a great many weights having been found in it. It was perhaps more probably the warehouse of a scale-maker. These weights were made of marble, basalt, or lead, and were for the most part round; but they had often the shape of the articles sold in the shop, as may be seen in some specimens in the museum at Naples. The weight was inscribed upon them. Some of the leaden ones were square, and had engraved upon them the words, EME ET HABEBIS: "buy and you shall have." On the right hand side of the street, or that towards the sea, are some houses of the kind we have already described, having the higher story on a level with the street, with two more stories below.　Here also is the house called the *Casa delle Danzatrici,* or the house of the female dancers, from some pictures which it contained.

After passing these objects, we arrive at a point where another little street, or rather lane, called the *Vicolo di Narcisso,* diverges from the *Strada Consolare,* and running more directly north, forms an acute angle with it. At the point of junction, called by the Romans *bivium,* is a fountain, and behind it a low square vaulted erection, which is sometimes supposed to have been a public cistern for supplying it.　The annexed cut will convey

an idea of it.　The circumstance of there being a door in one of the sides of the building militates against the notion of its having been a reservoir; but to what other purpose it may have been applied it is impossible to say.　The figures painted on this building, now entirely effaced, represented a

FOUNTAIN IN TRIVIIS NEAR THE GATE OF HERCULANEUM.

sacrifice to the *Lares Compitales,* or deities who presided over the highways; to whom also was dedicated a small altar that stands beneath.

Resuming our walk along the *Strada Consolare,* we come to a bakehouse on the left, adjoining the house of Sallust.　As may naturally be supposed, shops of this sort are of frequent recurrence at Pompeii, though some of the larger houses are provided with private bakeries.　All of them very much resemble one another, differing only in size.　One or two of them show, by the comfortable air of the attached dwelling, that the proprietor must have been a well-to-do man.　The annexed photograph represents that which we have just mentioned.　In the background is the oven with the furnace underneath, and at the side of the wall two mills for grinding the corn; for there seems to have been no separate trade of a miller at Pompeii.　The mills here depicted may serve to explain the whole process.　In the one in front, the lower millstone only is seen, in the shape of a cone.　The upper millstone, a large fragment of which may be seen on the further mill, was fitted exactly on this, by means of a strong iron pivot on the top of the

MILLS AND OVEN.

cone. This upper stone was somewhat in the shape of an hour-glass, having both its ends hollow; one for the purpose of covering the cone, the other to serve as a hopper for receiving the corn. At the point of junction of these two parts was an iron socket, intended to revolve on the pivot of the cone: while round the outside of this narrowest part ran a strong iron band, with two square holes, into which were inserted bars of wood for turning the mill, either by manual labour, or, when the mill was large, by that of animals. The annexed cut is from an antique bas-relief in terra-cotta, representing a mule attached to a mill. The corn inserted in the upper cone, or hopper, gradually worked its way to the bottom, and came out on the cylindrical base in the shape of flour. The work was laborious and degrading, and was therefore commonly performed by slaves, as we see from frequent allusions in the ancient comic writers; and sometimes, like the tread-mill, by way of punishment. Frequently, however, and especially in Greece, this work seems to have been assigned to women. This primitive fashion is still kept up at Naples, where numerous shops of dealers in flour may be seen

ANTIQUE BAS-RELIEF IN TERRA-COTTA, REPRESENTING A MULE ATTACHED TO A MILL.

having a large hand-mill, though of a different construction from the ancient one. Such shops have invariably a picture of the Madonna, intended perhaps as a security for the good faith of the dealer; though this practice sometimes obtains in other shops. Many loaves have been discovered in the ovens of Pompeii, of course in a carbonised state, yet otherwise so perfect that on some of them stamped inscriptions may still be read, indicating the sort of corn of which the loaf was made. They are of a cake-like appearance, flat, and about eight inches in diameter. They appear very often to have been baked in moulds, of which several have been found.

BREAD DISCOVERED IN POMPEII.

The excavations have also taught us the ancient method of conducting the trade of a fuller. Just opposite the eastern side of Pansa's house is a fuller's workshop, called the *Fullonica*, on the walls of which were paintings representing the operations of the trade. The first operation was that of washing. This was done in vats, in which the cloths were trodden and well

FULLER AT WORK, FROM A PAINTING IN THE FULLONICA.

worked by the feet of the scourers, as represented in the annexed cut, taken from the walls of the Fullonica. Their dress, which consisted of two tunics,

CARDING A TUNIC, FROM A PAINTING IN THE FULLONICA.

the upper one green, the under one yellow, is tucked up so as to leave the legs bare. Three of the figures seem to have finished their work, and to be wringing the articles on which they have been employed; the fourth, resting his arms on a low wall, appears to be jumping and working about the contents of his vat with his feet. When dry, the cloth was brushed and carded to raise the nap; after which it was fumigated with sulphur, and bleached in the sun. The second cut represents a man brushing or carding a tunic suspended from a rope. Another man carries a frame

and pot, meant probably for fumiga-
tion and bleaching; the cloths being spread upon the frame, and the
pot containing live coals and sulphur, placed under it. This man
is thought to have an olive garland
on his head, while the owl upon the
frame is the bird sacred to Minerva,
the tutelar goddess of manual labour.
At the left hand corner, a female,
apparently, from her dress, a person
of condition, or it may be the mis-
tress of the establishment, is examining a piece of cloth presented
to her by a girl. The third cut
represents a clothpress, which is
also depicted on the walls.

CLOTHPRESS, FROM A PAINTING IN THE FULLONICA.

There are indications at Pompeii of various other trades, though we
cannot, as in the two preceding instances, trace the methods of conducting
them. Thus in the Street of the Tombs, on the left hand side, is a potter's;
in the Strada Consolare, not far from the second fountain, is a cartwright's, and
at no great distance a soap manufactory; in the Street of Fortune, nearly
opposite to the House of the Faun, dwelt a maker of plaster casts; at the
corner of the Street of the Augustales and that of the Lupanari was the shop
of a shoemaker, identified by the tools which it contained; a painted sign on
the house at the corner of the Street of Mercury and the Vicoletto of the
same name has led to the idea that it belonged to an incense dealer and per-
fumer. Besides these have been discovered a dyer's, a chemical laboratory,
two or three apothecary's shops, a barber's, a colour shop, a sculptor's, an
oil-dealer's, a goldsmith's, a stonemason's, &c. In fact, most of the modern
trades are represented in this ancient Roman town.

We will now resume our progress up the Strada Consolare. Next to the
bakery before described is the house called, though for no very satisfactory
reason, the House of Sallust. It is not one of the largest class of houses,
yet in point of decoration it may rank among the most elegant in Pompeii.
Beyond this we pass another and a larger bakery, one of the most extensive

in Pompeii, and next to it what is called the *Casa della Academia di Musica*, or house of the Academy of Music. On the right hand side of the way, opposite to this, is the house of Julius Polybius, also one of the noticeable ones in Pompeii.

We are now arrived at a point where the street forks into two branches. That on the right, called *Vico del Farmacista*, is an unimportant bye street, whilst the other, the continuation of the main line, verging a little to the left, conducts into the *Strada delle Terme*, or Street of the Baths, and so towards the Forum. Arrived at the corner of the *Strada delle Terme* we will turn round for a moment and survey the prospect before us, as depicted in the accompanying photograph, taken, though of course at a considerable elevation, from a spot near this point.

The street on the left hand side of the picture is that which we have just ascended; that which forms a sharp angle with it, and recedes before us into the distance, is the lane called *Vicolo di Modesto*, after a house of the same name that stands in it. The rounded corner at the nearest end of this

shows where the main street, or *Strada Consolare*, runs into the Street of the Baths. At the angle of the two first-named streets stands another fountain, but without any *castellum*, or reservoir, behind it. So abundant were these public fountains that most of the streets were provided with one. Towards the right of the picture, in the middle distance, may be seen the columns belonging to the peristyle of the house of Pansa; while still further to the right, and nearer to the spectator, may be seen the entrance to the house, marked by two square pilasters, that on the right still perfect and having a capital somewhat resembling the Corinthian order. The annexed cut, made many years

VIEW OF THE ENTRANCE TO THE HOUSE OF PANSA.

VIEW NEAR THE OLD BATHS.

ago, will show their appearance when more perfect. Over the buildings is seen the distant landscape, closed by the noble forms of Vesuvius.

The house of Pansa was one of the largest and handsomest in Pompeii. It occupied the whole of what the Romans called an *insula*—that is, a space surrounded on every side by streets, as an island is by water. It was of an oblong form, in length about three hundred feet, including the garden, whilst the breadth of its frontage towards the Street of the Baths was about one hundred feet. It was on the usual plan of a Roman house, being entered from the street by a vestibule followed by a narrow *prothyrum*, or passage, having on the floor the inscription SALVE in mosaic. This led into the atrium—a quadrangular space having a large square opening in the roof, called the *compluvium*, through which the rain water, carried down by the slanting of the roof, fell into a basin below, generally of marble. At the sides of the atrium were small rooms, probably intended for guests. Beyond these are open recesses on each side called *alæ*, or wings, forming part of the area of the atrium. Opposite the entrance is the apartment called tablinum, which seems to have been designed for a sort of office or place of business. It was an open room, allowing a passage through it into the peristyle beyond, though capable of being closed by means of a curtain or of wooden paneling. This apartment was often handsomely decorated with paintings, a mosaic floor, &c. By the side of it was a narrow passage called the *fauces*, or jaws, the usual way for passing from the atrium into the peristyle, and indeed the only one when the tablinum was closed. Two apartments contiguous to the tablinum, and like it standing between the atrium and peristyle, may have been used as libraries or studies. The view given further on of the house of Cornelius Rufus will enable the reader to realize the arrangement we have described. In this view the foreground shows part of the atrium with the *impluvium*. The open apartment in the middle, to the right of the bust, is the *tablinum*, while beyond are seen the columns of the peristyle. This last was a large court not unlike the atrium in appearance and arrangement, but larger and more handsomely decorated. The large oblong basin in the middle of that of the house of Pansa was surrounded with sixteen columns, forming the roofed portico which encompassed the peristyle. The basin, or *piscina*, was usually adorned with a handsome fountain, of which we shall have to speak further on, and had at its sides one or two wells. But sometimes the place of the basin was filled with a small garden, or rather flower-bed, called *xystus*. On the left of the peristyle were bedchambers for the family; on the right was a large *triclinium* or dining-room. At the further extremity of the peristyle, and facing the *tablinum*, was a spacious and handsomely decorated apartment, the finest in the house, which probably served as a drawing-room or reception-room. Such a room was called *œcus*, a house, probably from its size. At the sides of this were several smaller apartments, into the destination of which we need not here enter, while beyond, extending across the whole breadth of the building, was a portico of two stories, which led into a large square garden. On the left hand side of the *œcus* was a large room with an opening to the street, which has been sometimes called an *ergastulum*, or work-room for the slaves, and sometimes a stable. Adjoining this is the kitchen. It had a stove still containing charcoal for

stews, &c, represented in the annexed woodcut. Before it lie a knife, a strainer, and an instrument meant perhaps for a frying-pan or for cooking eggs. In the kitchen was a curious painting representing a sacrifice to the Lares, or household deities. Below are the holy serpents, frequently depicted in honour of them, licking the offering from the altar. At the sides

STOVE IN THE KITCHEN OF THE HOUSE OF PANSA.

are represented various eatables, as a group of small birds, a string of fish, a hare or rabbit, a pig with a girt round its body, a few loaves or cakes, re-

sembling in form those which we have already described as having been found in Pompeii, an eel spitted on a wire, a ham, or a leg of mutton, a boar's head, and what appears to be a loin of pork, or of some other meat.

We have now described the more striking features of the house of Pansa; to enter into minute details, which would be unintelligible without a ground-plan,

RELIGIOUS PAINTING IN THE KITCHEN OF THE HOUSE OF PANSA.

would be out of place in a work like the present. The arrangements of the house of Pansa serve to convey a good general idea of a first-class private house at Pompeii, though there are of course often divergencies in the details. Further down, in the same line of street, is a sister-house, that of the Faun, so called from an admirable little statuette of a dancing Faun, one of the bijoux of Pompeian sculpture, which graced its fountain. This house, like that of Pansa, fills an entire *insula* of about the same dimensions, and appears to have been entirely in the occupation of the owner, while part of Pansa's house seems to have been let out for shops and lodgings. The house of the Faun, besides other minor differences, has two distinct *atria*, and the peristyle has its longer side across the breadth instead of the depth of the house. The garden, too, is completely surrounded by a portico, which still contains upwards of a hundred *amphoræ*, or wine-jars; whence it has been conjectured that the owner was a wine merchant. It was a common practice enough for the owners of these large mansions to let out parts of them that adjoined the street. A considerable portion of the right hand side of that of Pansa, forming three distinct small houses with several rooms, as well as two shops, one on each side of the entrance, were evidently occupied by persons unconnected with the family, as there is no communication between these portions and the house. In other shops having such a communication the proprietor probably carried on a trade that was superintended by his slaves. The house of the Faun had also one shop of this description, where perhaps the owner sold his wine.

Before we quit the house of Pansa we may remark that Mazois, many years ago, thought that he had discovered at one of the side entrances a Christian emblem in the sign of a cross, worked in bas-relief on a panel of white stucco. The bas-relief has now disappeared, but the inference of Mazois seems untenable for several reasons. First, because the Christians do not appear to have adopted the cross as an emblem till a much later period; secondly, because, even if they had then adopted it, they would hardly have dared to display it so publicly in those days of persecution, and still less would they have done so in combination with the Pagan emblems which are said to have accompanied this cross. That there were Christians in Pompeii may be easily believed, but not that they should have ventured openly to proclaim their creed. It is more credible that inscriptions may have been found in which they are taunted and abused. It is said that an imperfect one of this sort has been found, written with coal or charcoal on the walls of a house in the *Vico dei Lupanari*. The only letters visible were . . . . *ni gaude . . . . hristiane*, which has been supplemented *igni gaude, Christiane:* "enjoy your fire, Christian;" in allusion to the burning of the Christians under Nero.

These and other like inscriptions—we are not speaking of those cut in stone—afford us a peep both into the political and the domestic life of the Pompeians. Advertisements of a political character are commonly painted on the exterior walls in large letters in red and black paint; poetical effusions and pasquinades are often in chalk or coal (Martial, *Epp.*, xii. 61, 9); while notices of a domestic kind are more usually found in the interior of the houses, scratched with a sharp point, such as a nail or knife on the stucco of the walls or pillars, and are hence called *graffiti*; and sometimes, as in the instance just mentioned, written with charcoal. The many political inscriptions bear testimony to the activity of public life in Pompeii. Numerous advertisements respecting the election of ædiles and other magistrates seem to show that the Pompeians, at the time when their city was destroyed, were in all the excitement of the *comitia*, which were approaching for the creation of such magistrates. We shall here select a few of the more interesting inscriptions of both kinds from those collected by Overbeck in the second volume of his valuable work on Pompeii (chap. vi).

It seems to have been the practice to paint over old advertisements with a coating of white in order to obtain a fresh surface for new ones; just as a bill-sticker in London pastes his bill over that of some predecessor. In many instances the new coat has been detached or fallen off, thus revealing an older notice belonging sometimes to a period antecedent to the Social War. Such inscriptions are only found on the solid stone pillars of the more ancient buildings, and not on the stucco with which, at a later period, almost everything was plastered. Their antiquity is further revealed by the circumstance that some of them are in the Oscan dialect; while those in Latin are distinguished from more recent ones in the same language by the forms of the letters, by the names which appear in them, and by archaisms in orthography and grammar. Inscriptions in the Greek tongue are few, though letters of the Greek alphabet scratched on walls at a little height from the ground, and thus evidently the work of schoolboys, show that Greek must have been extensively taught at Pompeii.

The normal form of the electioneering advertisements contains the name of the person recommended, the office for which he is a candidate, and the name of the person or persons who recommend him; the latter generally accompanied with the formula ovf. From examples written in full, recently discovered, it appears that these letters mean *orat* (or *orant*) *vos faciatis*, "beseech you to create" (*ædile* and so forth.) The letters in question were, before this discovery, very often thought to stand for *orat ut faveat*, "begs him to favour;" and thus the meaning of the inscription was entirely reversed, the person recommending being converted into the person recommended. For instance, in the following example: *M. Holconium Priscum duumvirum juri dicendo O. V. F. Philippus:* the meaning will be, according to the older interpretation, "Philippus beseeches M. Holconius Priscus, Duumvir Justice, to favour (or patronize) him;" whereas the true sense is, "Philippus beseeches you to create M. Holconius Priscus a Duumvir of Justice." From this misinterpretation names have often been wrongly given to houses. Thus the house of Pansa has been so named from the following inscription in red letters, which might formerly be read on one of the pilasters of his doorway: "Pansam: aed: Paratus, rogat;" meaning "Paratus solicits you to make Pansa aedile;" the words *rogat*, or *petit*, "asks" or "requests" being sometimes substituted for *orat;* the inscription in this case being in a very abbreviated form, yet, from the well-known tenour of such advertisements, quite intelligible to a Pompeian. Such being the meaning, and not that Paratus solicits the favour of Pansa—and indeed it would have been a bad way to gain it by disfiguring his walls in so impertinent a manner—it seems probable that the house belonged to Paratus the recommender rather than Pansa the recommendee, and that he posted on his own walls a request to passers-by to make his friend Pansa aedile. Had it been the house of Pansa, when a candidate for the aedileship, and if it was the custom for such candidates to post recommendatory notices on their doors, it may be supposed that Pansa's would have exhibited more than this single one from a solitary friend. We do not mean to deny that adulatory inscriptions were sometimes written on the houses or doors of powerful or popular men or pretty women. That such was the custom we learn from a verse of Plautus (impleantur meae fores elogiorum carbonibus, *Mercator*, act ii. sc. 3: "My doors would be filled with praises in charcoal"). But first, the inscription on the house in question was evidently not one of the adulatory, but recommendatory, kind; and secondly, those of the former description, as we also learn from this passage, seem to have been written by a passing admirer with some material ready to the hand, as a piece of charcoal, and not painted on the walls with care, and time, and expense—a mode of proceeding which we can hardly think that the owner of the house, if he was a man of sense and modesty, would have tolerated.

Recommendations of candidates were often accompanied with a word or two in their praise, as *dignus*, or *dignissimus est*, *probissimus*, *juvenis integer*, *omni bono meritus*, &c., that is, he is worthy, or very worthy, a most excellent man, a young man of integrity, in every way deserving, &c. These recommendations are sometimes subscribed by guilds or corporations, and show that there were a great many of these trade unions at Pompeii. Thus we find mentioned the *offectores*, or dyers, the *pistores* (bakers), *aurifices* (goldsmiths), *pomarii* (fruiterers), *coparii* (greengrocers), *lignarii* (wood merchants), *plostrarii* (cartmakers), *piscicapi* (fishermen), *agricolæ* (husbandmen), *muliones* (muleteers), *culinarii* (cooks), *fullones* (fullers), &c. Advertisements of this sort seem to have been laid hold of, as a vehicle for street wit, just as electioneering squibs are perpetrated among ourselves. Thus we find mentioned, as among the companies, the *pilicrepi* (ball-players), the *seribibi* (latedrinkers), the *dormientes universi* (all the worshipful company of sleepers); and, as a climax, *Pompeiani universi* (every man of the Pompeians votes for so and so). One of these recommendations, purporting to emanate from a " teacher," or " professor," runs, *Valentius, cum discentes suos* (Valentius with his disciples); the bad grammar being probably intended as a gibe upon one of the poor man's weak points.

The *graffiti*, and occasionally the painted inscriptions, contain sometimes well-known verses from poets still extant. Some of these exhibit variations from the modern text; but, being written by not very highly educated persons, they seldom or never present any various readings that it would be desirable to adopt, and indeed contain now and then prosodiacal errors. Other verses, and some by no means contemptible, are either taken from pieces that are now lost, or are the invention of the writer himself. Many of these inscriptions are of course of an amatory character; some convey intelligence of not much importance to any but the writer; as that he is troubled with a cold, or that he considers somebody who does not invite him to supper as no better than a brute and barbarian, or invokes blessings on the man that does. Some are capped by another hand with a biting sarcasm on the first writer; and many, as might be expected, are scurrilous and indecent. Now and then the *graffiti* on the interior walls and pillars of houses are memorandums of domestic affairs; as how many pounds of lard have been bought; how many tunics sent to be washed; when a child, or a donkey, was born, and the like. One of this description, found scratched on the wall of the peristyle of the corner house in the *Strada della Fortuna* and *Vicolo dei Scienziati*, is an account of the spinning-tasks allotted to the female slaves, and is interesting as furnishing us with the names of several of them, viz: Vitalis, Florentina, Amarullis, Januaria, Heracla, Maria (Mária, feminine of Marius, not María), Lalagia (reminding us of Horace's Lalage), Damalis, and Doris.

Besides the *graffiti* in letters, there are also caricatures and rude drawings, with the names affixed, or an explanation of the meaning of the picture, which in some cases is very necessary. Figures of gladiators are one of the favourite subjects of these wall artists. But to describe all these inscriptions would almost demand a volume to itself, and we must now resume the thread of our description.

The shops of Pompeii, both those connected with the mansions and those of a more tradesman-like kind, were small and mean. The best seem to have been in the Street of Abundance, also called the Street of the Silversmiths, leading out of the south-east corner of the Forum; but a tradesman of London or Paris, or even of a good provincial town, would turn up his nose at them. At the angle of the two streets, just behind the fountain shown in the photographic view, was a small shop, called by some a thermopolium, or shop for the sale of hot drinks. The walls were gaudily painted in blue panels with red borders, and towards the street was a counter cased with marble. The stains left on these counters, apparently by wet drinking-glasses, have led to the identification, or supposed identification, of several such shops. A curious vessel for making these warm drinks has been discovered. It somewhat resembles a modern urn, as will be seen from the accompanying cut of it, but is much more complicated. The annexed

URN FOR WARM DECOCTIONS DRANK IN THE THERMOPOLIA.

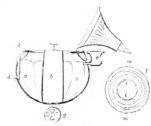

SECTION OF THE URN.

figure shows a section of the urn with its conical cover; a a is the body of the urn, b a small cylindrical furnace in the centre. It has four holes

H

in the bottom, as shown on the plan at *g*, meant to let the ashes fall through, and to create a draught; *c*, a vase-shaped mouth, by means of which the water was poured in, serving also for the escape of steam; *d*, a tube, which, by means of a cock, served to let off the fluid. It is placed thus high to prevent the pipe being stopped up by the ingredient decocted; *e* is a conical cover, the hollow of which is closed by a thin plate somewhat concave; *f*, a moveable flat cover with a hole in the middle, which closes the whole urn except the mouth of the small furnace; *m m*, nuts and screws which fasten the moveable cover on the rim of the urn; *i i*, rim, convex on the outside and concave within, which, the cover being put on, receives into its concavity the rim of the mouth of the furnace.

While on the subject of shops, we will briefly describe a cook's shop in the quarter of the theatres, represented in a restored form in the annexed cut. The front is entirely open to the street and displays a counter, before

A COOK'S SHOP.

which a customer is standing. The front was closed at night with shutters sliding in grooves in the lintel and basement wall. The counter has several large jars let into it, calculated to hold oil, olives, pickles, &c. At the further end of the counter is a small oven, probably for keeping some favourite dishes warm. All the details of the view are taken from objects existing or depicted at Pompeii. At the right hand top corner may be again seen the sacred serpent.

The general narrowness of the streets of Pompeii may be inferred from those seen in the preceding view; where, however, it will also be perceived that they were commonly provided with trottoirs. The convenience of the foot passengers was also consulted by placing large stepping-stones for crossing. In the narrower streets or lanes one of these sufficed; for three or four steps brought a man from one wall to the other; but in the broader streets may be seen three stepping-stones or even four. The wheels of the carriages passed at the sides of the stones, while the horses probably stepped over. From the few remains of horses or carriages discovered at Pompeii it may be inferred that its streets were not so encumbered with this sort of traffic as those of a modern town of the same class. Pompeii, however, standing on the road to southern Italy, must have been a considerable thoroughfare; to which, indeed, the deep ruts visible in some of its streets, and even marks of the iron tyres of the wheels, bear satisfactory evidence. The narrowness of the streets, especially as the houses were not very lofty, must have been rather agreeable than otherwise in that hot climate, as calculated to afford more shade. In some of the lanes the view of the sky must have been almost excluded by the projecting *mæniana*, or balconies. We may judge of their effect by the restoration of one effected by the Commendatore Fiorelli, the present director of the excavations, in the street called after it, *Vico del Balcone Pensile*, the only example in the place.

Nearly opposite to the main entrance to the house of Pansa stands one of the public baths, excavated in the year 1824. These establishments are a characteristic feature of ancient life, to which modern times can offer no parallel. At Rome especially they were ultimately carried to an extraordinary pitch of magnificence. The vast remains of the Baths of Caracalla and Diocletian that may be seen in that capital still strike the spectator with astonishment. But though these establishments provided accommodation for hundreds of bathers at once, this was only part of their attraction. They stood among extensive gardens and walks, and often were surrounded with a portico. Besides vast halls for swimming and bathing, they contained numerous others for conversation, for various athletic exercises, for the declamations of poets and the lectures of philosophers; in a word, for almost every species of polite and manly amusement.

We must not of course expect anything approaching these establishments in a provincial town like Pompeii, which perished too in an age when, even at Rome, the extent and splendour of the public baths had not yet attained

to the highest point of development.   Nevertheless, the baths of this third-
rate town cannot at present be matched in the most splendid capitals of
Europe.   They occupy a large space of ground, and offer, in two distinct
suites of elegant apartments, one designed for men, the other for women,
accommodation roomy enough for many persons to enjoy at once the cold,
the warm, or the tepid bath.   But beyond this no provision appears to have
been made in this set of baths for any other species of recreation.   Within
five or ten minutes' walk of them, however, is another and a larger set, first
discovered in 1858, and called the Thermæ Stabianæ, from one of the sides
of the building abutting on the street of that name.   These have in their
centre a spacious quadrangular court, partly surrounded with a portico,
which might have served as a *palæstra*, or place for wrestling and other
gymnastic exercises; whilst a long and narrow-paved strip on one side of it,
on which stood two large spheres of stone, appears to have been intended for
some game with the nature of which we are unacquainted.   On two sides of
the quadrangle, besides a large swimming bath open to the sky, were
several rooms suited for the accommodation of visitors, the outside walls of
which were adorned with paintings and well-executed reliefs in stucco.
Both the Pompeian *thermæ* are pretty similar in arrangement.   Each contains
both in the men's and women's divisions, an *apodyterium*, or undressing room,
a *frigidarium*, or cold bath, a *tepidarium*, or tepid bath, and a *caldarium*, or
warm and vapour bath, besides other apartments and necessary appurtenances,
such as furnaces and the like.   The bathing rooms are elegantly ornamented
with sculptures, paneled ceilings, bas-reliefs in stucco, &c.   We annex a cut of
a stucco ornament in the ceiling of the tepidarium in the smaller Thermæ.   It

STUCCO ORNAMENT IN THE CEILING OF THE TEPIDARIUM.

represents a winged child or genius guiding two dolphins, and followed by
another genius riding one sea-horse and accompanied by another.

The way is not long from the Old Baths to the Forum.   Keeping along

the street, called the *Strada delle Terme*, or Street of the Baths, which
runs between them and the house of Pansa, we soon arrive at another which
cuts it at right angles. The portion of it on our left is the *Strada di Mer-
curio*, or Street of Mercury, so called from a figure of Mercury in bas-
relief, stealing or bearing a purse, on one of the houses in it. It is a rather
long street, leading quite down to the town walls, some way to the east of
the gate of Herculaneum; it is straight, tolerably broad, and altogether one of
the handsomest streets in Pompeii. The houses that line its sides, or stand
in its immediate neighbourhood, are among the best in the town. The upper
end of it is spanned by a triumphal arch, on the top of which once stood a bronze
equestrian statue of Nero. It answered to another arch of the same description, which faces it at the entrance of the Forum. These arches have led to
the conjecture that it was the way of state into the city, and that formerly
there was at its termination a gate in the wall, which does not now appear.

The Street of Mercury is continued towards the Forum, by another
shorter, but rather broader, street, called the Street of the Forum, into
which it runs through the second triumphal arch. At the left, or north-
eastern corner of the street, stands a small temple, which must have been
pretty enough when perfect. It is identified, from inscriptions found in it,
to have been the Temple of Fortune, and is also connected in the same
manner with one M. Tullius, who erected it on his own ground, and with
his own money. There are no satisfactory means of connecting this person

VIEW OF THE TEMPLE OF FORTUNE.

with the celebrated orator, M. Tullius Cicero. The cut annexed will give
an idea of it in its present ruined state.

Proceeding down this short broad street, and passing through the triumphal arch, we find ourselves in the Forum. The photographic view annexed is taken from a spot at some distance beyond it, when the spectator, having turned round, again fronts the north and the distant Vesuvius. Through the archway is seen Nero's arch already mentioned, at the top of the Street of Mercury. The niches in the first arch were destined to hold statues. There are similar recesses towards the street on the other side, which appear to have held fountains as well as statues. This arch was doubtless also surmounted by a statue. The temple seen on the left of the arch has been called the Temple of Jupiter; but, as in most other cases, without any adequate authority for the appellation. In fact, of the nine temples of which remains exist at Pompeii, two only, that of Fortune, already mentioned, and that of Isis, are certainly known, from inscriptions found in them, to have been dedicated to the divinities whose names they bear.

The Temple of Jupiter is *prostyle*, or having a pseudo-dipteral portico with six columns in the front of the Corinthian order, and four columns at the sides, reckoning again the corner ones, and making in the whole twelve columns; but for the most part only the lower portions of these columns remain, as seen in the view. They are of lava, covered with stucco. There are on each side of the interior of the *cella*, the front, and one of the side walls of which are seen in the view, a row of eight apparently Ionic columns, originally between sixteen and seventeen feet high. Over these again was another row of Corinthian columns, some of the capitals of which have been found. The lower columns supported a gallery to which there was access by stairs at the back of the temple; while the higher ones are supposed by some to have supported a light roof of painted wood; though others think, perhaps not so probably, that the temple was *hypæthral*, or open to the sky. At the further end of the cell are three small chambers for the service of the priests, or they might have served for the public treasury. The clear length of the cell between these chambers and the portico was about forty-two feet, with a breadth of twenty-eight feet and a-half. In this cell was the statue of the deity. The journals of the excavations record there having been found in it, January 21st, 1817, several fragments of a colossal marble statue, and a colossal head, in alabaster, of a Jupiter, beautifully executed; a discovery which strengthens the supposition that the temple may have been dedicated to that deity. The interior of the cell was painted, black and red being the predominant colours. The pavement consisted of diamond-shaped pieces of marble, enclosed in a broad border of black and

VIEW IN THE FORUM.

white mosaic. In the centre of the door-sill are traces of bolts for folding doors. The temple, as will be seen, is placed on a lofty basement, or podium, ascended by many steps; a feature which essentially distinguishes the temples of Pompeii from those of Greece. That it was of a later date, and built after the Roman occupation, is shown by the stucco on the pillars; with which indeed most of the buildings round the Forum are covered. There are the remains of an ancient temple in the Greek style, evidently belonging to the early days of Pompeii, in the place called the Triangular Forum, near the theatres, at the southern extremity of the town. It is in a very dilapidated state, but there are remains enough to make out the method of its construction. Its style is the pure Grecian Doric, resembling that of the celebrated temple at Pæstum, and the columns are of solid stone. This building, however, is also placed upon a podium; a method which, by raising the floor to a level with the eye, brought at once the whole order into view, from the stylobate or platform of the columns to the roof. In the case of the temple of Jupiter, a side door in the basement, formed by the podium, led to vaults beneath the temple.

On the right hand side of the triumphal arch another arch gave access for foot passengers to the pavement and portico which surrounded the Forum. On the extreme right of the view is seen the entrance to a large temple, which has been very commonly called the Pantheon; but was more probably the temple of Augustus. The former name was derived from twelve pedestals placed in a circle in the middle of the large area which the visitor enters, on which are supposed to have stood statues of the twelve greater gods. But, not to mention that this would have been a somewhat odd arrangement, and that we should rather have expected to see the shrines of these aristocratic deities ranged round the sides of the building, as in the Pantheon at Rome—which, however, did not contain the twelve Magni Dii—so that each might receive with more majesty and decorum the adoration of his worshippers, the pedestals themselves do not seem fitted for the reception of statues, and especially of those of such mighty divinities. Nor are the chambers or cells on the south side of the building supposed to have been those of the priests of these deities, twelve in number, but only eleven. Overbeck, therefore, seems rightly to have concluded that the objects in question were no pedestals, but pediments for supporting some light wooden roof or building, though we cannot agree with him that it might have been a temple of Vesta; a notion which seems to have been suggested merely by its circular form. But, even allowing that this was a temple at all, other deities beside Vesta had round temples, and all the accessories of the building seem in the highest degree inappropriate to the vestal worship. It appears more probable that the building was dedicated to the worship of Augustus. The chambers and ædiculæ at the further side of the building contained statues of members of the imperial family, and one no doubt of Augustus himself, to which may have belonged the fragment discovered of an arm holding a globe. The Augustals, or priests of Augustus, were a distinguished body, or corporation, at Pompeii, as is evident from the frequent mention of them in inscriptions, and such a building as the present would have been a suitable place for their meetings and festivals. Such corporations, whether priestly or otherwise, are never averse to good living; and the numerous paintings of eatables and delicacies round

FROM THE PAINTINGS ON THE WALLS OF THE PANTHEON.

the walls of this temple, show that its priests formed no exception to the remark. We have already given from these pictures a representation of Cupids making bread; we now subjoin others of lobsters, fruit, birds, and other articles.

In front of this building, under the portico of the Forum, were seven small shops, the lower part of the walls of which may still be seen in our view. They were probably *tabernæ argentariæ*, or shops of money-changers; a view which is corroborated by there having been found in one of them, in a box almost destroyed, between 1200 and 1300 silver and brass coins. The pedestals of some of the tables still remain. Still further in front, at the edge of the foot-pavement, may be seen one of the pillars of the portico of the Forum; and on a line with it, several pedestals which appear to have supported statues.

From the point of view whence the preceding photograph is taken, only a small portion of the Forum, forming its north-eastern corner, can be seen. To obtain a better prospect, we should proceed to its southern end, when facing round to the north, the whole area lies before us. When the Forum and its buildings were in a perfect state, the view must have been very beautiful and striking. Even in superficial size it is not much surpassed by the Forum Romanum, or original Forum of Rome, while its situation is far superior. Sunk in a deep hollow between the surrounding hills at the very lowest level in the city, the prospect from the Roman Forum was of the most confined description, though doubtless this defect must have been partly compensated by the aspect of the magnificent buildings with which the hills were lined and crowned. The Forum of Pompeii, on the contrary, occupies one of the most elevated sites in the town, and commands magnificent views of the surrounding country. On the north rises Vesuvius with its two summits, from the higher one of which wreaths of smoke are continually ascending. On the south are seen Mount St. Angelo and Mount Lactarius, gradually sinking down towards Cape Campanella, the southernmost boundary of the Gulf. Nor was the Forum of Pompeii deficient in architectural grandeur. When all that area was paved with pure white marble—of which only a few isolated slabs now remain—when numerous statues, some of them equestrian, stood on those dilapidated pedestals, the *coup-d'œil* must have been sufficiently striking. And as the ground-plans *in toto*, partly also the elevations of the temples and other buildings which surround it are still perfect, there is at present no spot more calculated to

I

awaken reminiscences of ancient public life. It requires no great effort
of the imagination to restore the spot to its pristine state, and to repeople
it with its accustomed throng of occupants, partly men of business, partly
loungers. We may call up in fancy the bustling crowd of buyers and sellers
in the cloth market at the south-east corner, commonly called the Chalcidicum, or edifice of Eumachia; the members of the long robe and their
clients in the vast Basilica which faces it; the Augustales, those aldermen
of ancient times, preparing to feast on the choicest viands in the temple of
Augustus or the Pantheon; other citizens, as fancy led or vows compelled,
offering a sacrifice in the temple of Jupiter, or Mercury, or Venus; while those
who had no particular call either of business or devotion, seeking shelter from
the noontide sun under the spacious porticos, sauntered leisurely to and fro,
discussing the price of corn or wine, or the latest news from Rome, or set-
tling the approaching election of ædiles, or speculating on the event of the
next gladiatorial combat.

Before we quit the Forum, we must inspect it a little more minutely.

The porticos of which we have spoken consist of a Grecian Doric colonnade, which runs uninterruptedly around the west, south, and east sides
of the Forum. The columns are twelve feet high, and two feet three or
four inches in diameter. They were set aræostyle, that is, wide apart, the
distance between them being about three and a-half diameters, or eight feet
and a-half. In this method of construction it was difficult to find pieces of
stone long enough to reach from one pillar to another and form the archi-
traves; so that it became necessary either to make these of wood, or to

construct a flat arch. The former method was
adopted at Pompeii, and a stone entablature raised
upon the wood, as shown in the annexed cut. Above
this there was probably a gallery, the circuit of
which, however, must in some instances have been
interrupted by the porticos of the adjacent buildings. When this was the case, it has been supposed that stairs ran up to the gallery, or that
there may have been some mode of passing without descending to the ground. On the eastern
side are remains of an older arcade, which at the
time of the eruption the inhabitants were replac-

CONSTRUCTION IN WOOD AND STONE OF
THE ARÆOSTYLE PORTICO OF
THE FORUM.

ing with the portico. The pillars of the latter were of three materials, of fine white caserta stone, of an ancient yellowish tufa, and of brick plastered.

We will now proceed to examine the remaining buildings which surround the Forum. On the eastern side, that which stands next to the Pantheon, or Temple of Augustus, already described, has by some been thought to be a temple dedicated to three divinities, the inference being drawn from three recesses, designed apparently for statues, in three sides of the building. The opinion of those, however, seems more probable who hold that it was a Senaculum, or council-hall of the Decurions, the municipal senate. Little remains of it but the outside walls, built of brick mostly in the method called *opus reticulatum* (the bricks being set edge-ways, so as to give the wall a net-like appearance), and some columns of the same material, which were formerly covered with marble and stucco. The size of it well adapts it for a senate-hall, its spacious area being eighty-three feet by sixty : an altar stands in the centre, on which perhaps sacrifice was offered before the debates of the Council began, as we know was the custom in the Curia at Rome; where the statue of Victory, to which these sacrifices were made, became in the declining days of the empire so bitter a subject of contention between the Pagan and the Christian senators. The altar, from its position, does not seem to favour the idea that it could have ministered to the statues of divinities placed in the three recesses. Of these, however, the two on each side, near the entrance, contain each a large basis apparently meant for the statues of gods; while other smaller niches in the walls may have been intended for statues of the emperors, or of deserving citizens. The building terminates at the end opposite the entrance in an *apsis*, or semicircular recess, in which there is a raised seat, probably intended for the president of the assembly and the chief magistrates. On one side of this recess is a chamber which may have served for records. The pavement was composed of slabs of marble of different colours, symmetrically arranged, but of which there only remains a piece in the middle. The front of the portico of this edifice, composed of fluted white marble columns of the Ionic order, ranged even with the pillars of the portico of the Forum, without interrupting the promenade below.

The building next to that just described is undoubtedly a temple. It comprises an almost square area, fifty-seven feet and a-half, by about fifty feet and a-half, at the further end of which, elevated on a podium, is a small chapel, or *sacellum*. Steps on each side of the basement lead to the platform of the *cella;* at the further end of which is a basis for the statue of the deity.   In the middle of the area, in front of the chapel, is an altar of white marble, with an unfinished bas-relief representing a sacrifice.   The sacrificer appears to be a magistrate; he has a wreath round his head, which is also partly covered with his robes.   In his hand is a patera, with which apparently to sprinkle and purify the victim before it is offered up.   This figure has sometimes been imagined to represent Cicero, from a fancied likeness to the great orator; an idea springing from a natural desire to identify the objects which, after so many centuries, the excavations have brought to light.   The victim is led by the *popa,* or man whose office it was to kill it. He is naked to the waist, and bears the sacrificial axe (*malleus*).   A boy holding a vase and patera, the sacred *vitta,* or fillet, hanging from his neck, follows the principal personage.   Near him is a figure holding a patera that seems to be filled with bread, whilst another figure is sounding the tibia or double flute.   Behind are lictors; and in the back is represented a temple, decorated with garlands, before which the sacrifice is offered.   On the side of the altar opposite to this is a bas-relief of a wreath of oak-leaves, bound with a fillet, with a young olive tree on each side; while the other two sides are decorated with sculptures of instruments used in sacrifice, as shown in the annexed cut.   These consist of a patera, a vase, a *vitta* or fillet, an

ORNAMENTS OF SACRIFICE ON THE SIDES OF THE ALTAR.

incense box, a ladle, and a spiral instrument, the purpose of which is not precisely known, but which may have been used by the haruspex who inspected the entrails of the victim. The little chapel, or *sacellum,* is only about fifteen feet long by thirteen broad, so that it could contain little more than the statue of the deity.

The building, like others of the same kind, had apartments destined for the priests, in which numerous *amphoræ,* or wine jars, were discovered.   Those, however, as well as other articles, seen in the view, are the produce of different excavations: the Temple of Mercury having been converted into a temporary place of deposit for such articles as are not thought worthy of being carried to the Museum: and on this account it is closed with a railing.

The appellation of the Temple of Mercury, commonly given to this building, rests on no better foundation than that of the Temple of Jupiter.

It seems to have been vaguely drawn from a passage in Vitruvius, that the Temple of Mercury should be on the Forum. But if this name is uncertain, that of the Temple of Quirinus, which is sometimes given to it, is decidedly erroneous. This latter appellation was taken from an inscription on a basis which stands in front of the temple, commemorating the deeds of Romulus and his deification under the name of Quirinus. But as this pedestal was not found within the walls of the temple, but on a line with the colonnade of the Forum, and as an exactly similar one, with an inscription in honour of Æneas, stood on the other side of the Forum, exactly opposite to it, it is evident that they supported statues in honour of those two founders of the Roman race, and were in no way connected with the temples near them.

We now come to one of the largest public buildings in Pompeii, except of course the baths and the theatres. It embraces an area of about one hundred and thirty feet long, by sixty-five broad, having a peristyle and crypto-porticus on three of its sides; and in front, comprehending the footway of the Forum, a pseudo-dipteral portico of eighteen columns, supported on pedestals. The interior peristyle, or uninterrupted colonnade, consisted of admirably executed Corinthian columns of white marble, to judge by a small remaining portion of one pillar. Their total disappearance may be explained either by the Pompeians having returned and dug them up, or by their having been carried off by later emperors; a practice to which we have already alluded. Above the colonnade and crypto-porticus, there were probably wooden galleries. The cornice of the peristyle seems to have projected far over the interior area, and thus to have protected numerous little tables made of lava, on which it is conjectured that goods were displayed for sale. For over a side entrance in the Street of Abundance, which here turns down at right angles from the Forum, is an inscription stating that the crypto-porticus and a Chalcidicum were built at the expense of Eumachia, a public priestess; while at the further extremity of the building, and in that portion of it which is supposed to be the Chalcidicum, was a statue of Eumachia, and another inscription purporting that it was erected to her by the fullers; out of gratitude, we may presume, for her munificence in building this portico for their accommodation. Hence it has been concluded that the edifice was used as a market by the cloth manufacturers and fullers. We have already given some account of the latter trade as exercised at Pompeii. Ancient habits must have made this trade much more important among the Romans than it is now. When it is considered that wool formed almost the only material of their dresses, which, consequently, in a warm climate like Italy, must have often required a thorough purification,—not to mention the anxiety of a beau of small fortune to make his toga wear well and look well to the last,—we may readily imagine that the cloth manufacturer and the fuller must have had a large and lucrative trade; though in some cases, perhaps, the article was manufactured at home. Hence, we need not be surprised that so large a building was appropriated to the use of tradesmen of this description. It is generally called the edifice of Eumachia, sometimes also the Chalcidicum; though the latter name properly belonged, perhaps, only to the smaller portion of it in the rear.

The Street of Abundance, or of the Silversmiths, already mentioned as leading down by the side of this building, was one of the best and broadest in Pompeii, though inhabited apparently almost entirely by tradesmen. It is a peculiarity of the houses here that they have underground kitchens. The Street of Abundance was continued by a short but still broader street, called the Street of the Holconii, in which were situated the Stabian Baths already described. On the other side of the Street of Abundance, facing the edifice of Eumachia, and at the extreme south-eastern corner of the Forum, stood a building, the use of which cannot be determined, but which is sometimes thought to have been a school, and has obtained the name of the School of Verna. It has not, however, much the appearance of a school, the stone bench or counter in it seeming rather intended for the display of goods. Its name was taken from an inscription on the *album*, or whitened space for advertisements, which stood opposite to it on the wall of Eumachia's edifice; but which, from its situation, can of course prove nothing with respect to this building.

We are now arrived at the southern side of the Forum, or that which faces the temple of Jupiter. This side is entirely occupied by three buildings very similar both in size and plan. In the absence of all inscriptions or other means by which they might be identified, they have been supposed to be either *curiæ*, for the assemblies of magistrates, or courts of justice— wrongly called *tribunalia*—something like our police courts, for the trial of minor offences and causes. All that can be said with certainty is, that they are assuredly not temples, as they do not bear the slightest resemblance to any sacred building discovered at Pompeii. It has been sometimes conjectured that the middle one was an *ærarium*, or treasury; the only foundation, however, for which conjecture is that some two hundred loose pieces

62

THE BASILICA.

of coin were found in it! They seem to have been highly decorated with marble statues and columns, fragments of which, as well as pedestals for the statues, were found on the floors. Adjoining these buildings on the west, but not in the Forum, are some houses excavated by General Championnet.

At the south-west corner of the Forum, opposite to the so-called School of Verna, stands the Basilica, of which we give a photographic view. Its destination is clearly identified by its plan and arrangement, as well as, curiously enough, by the testimony of two ancient *graffiti* of its name on the walls, though somewhat mis-spelt (*bassilica*). Before we describe it, we will say a word or two on the origin and destination of such buildings.

The idea of a Basilica, as its Greek name implies, Βασιλική (στοά, sc., or οἰκία, a regal portico or building), was borrowed from the Greek, and the model of it was perhaps copied from the *regal portico* at Athens, where the magistrate called the *King Archon* sat to administer justice. The first building of the sort at Rome was erected by M. Porcius Cato, the censor, about the beginning of the second century, B.C., and was called, after him, the Basilica Porcia. It seems to have served both as a law court and a sort of exchange, and thus helped to relieve the Forum, the inconveniently small dimensions of which probably began about this time to make themselves felt. Cato's building was followed in a few years by two others, the Basilica Fulvia and the Basilica Sempronia. Several more were erected under the empire, of which the most celebrated are the Basilica Julia, the Basilica Ulpia, and that of Constantine. Of these three last there are still remains; but, with the exception of the Basilica Ulpia in the Forum of Trajan, where the broken pillars still remain much in the same fashion as in the Pompeian basilica, they are not so well calculated as that at Pompeii to give us an idea of this species of building.

With regard to its plan, a basilica was of an oblong form, and the rules of architecture required that its breadth should not be more than one half, nor less than one third, of its length. The basilica of Pompeii complies with this rule, being two hundred and twenty feet long, and eighty broad. Generally, on its lower columns rested smaller ones, supporting an upper gallery, and this also appears to have been the case at Pompeii. This latter basilica was entered through five doorways, approached by a flight of four steps. The peristyle supporting the roof consisted of twenty-eight large Ionic columns. The space between the peristyle and the exterior walls was thus converted into a covered gallery, over which, as we have said, ran an upper one, reached by a staircase outside the building. Overbeck, however, contends that there was no upper gallery, that the large Ionic pillars supported the roof, and that the staircase outside led not to the gallery of the basilica, but to that of the portico surrounding the Forum. The same author, however, is forced to admit that the engaged, or half-pillars, in the side walls, as seen in the view, which are considerably thinner than those which divide the nave and aisles, and which could scarcely have been more than half their height, seem to have helped to support a gallery; and that the existence of a gallery is further confirmed by the shafts, or fragments of the shafts, of smaller columns of the Corinthian order, with their capitals, having been found within the building, as well as the larger capitals of the Ionic pillars. At each corner of the building two pillars are joined together, which is supposed to be unique in Grecian architecture, and the earliest known example of that union of columns seen in a Gothic pier. It has also been disputed whether the basilica was *hypæthral*, and open to the sky, or roofed. The former supposition is rather favoured by the finding of *antefixa*, or sculptured ornaments, such as lions' heads, &c, which served to decorate the interior edge of a *compluvium*, or open roof.

A basilica usually had at the further extremity either a circular recess (*apsis*), or a square one. The absence of this in the building at Pompeii does not, however, militate against its having been a basilica, as there is ample room for the tribunal of the prætor or duumvir at the further extremity of the peristyle, where indeed it now stands. It is between six and seven feet high, and must have been ascended by wooden stairs. It was adorned with small columns, as seen in the view. In front is a pedestal on which were found the legs of a bronze statue. On each side of the tribunal was an apartment, intended probably for suitors and advocates, or for the officers of the court. Beneath the tribunal was a small dungeon or cellar, entered by stairs on each side, and lighted by two small apertures or vent holes. Its destination has not been ascertained, but it has been not improbably conjectured that it served as a temporary prison for accused persons.

The interior appears to have been richly decorated. The pavement was of marble, which, however, has been carried off, and only the pozzuolano remains, in which it was imbedded. Like many other buildings in Pompeii, it bears evident marks of having been anciently excavated. The pillars, however, are of brick coated with stucco. The interior walls were painted to resemble different coloured marbles; while the exterior is said to have been adorned, when first discovered, with grotesque architectural paintings, of which there are no longer any traces. As a court of justice, the basilica naturally sheltered a great many loiterers, not only suitors, witnesses, and others awaiting the coming on of a trial; but also persons attracted by curiosity, or seeking to kill time. Their presence was attested, when the stucco on the walls was perfect, by the numerous *graffiti* scratched upon it, which, however, with the exception of those carried to the Museum, have now almost entirely disappeared. In this respect the Pompeians resembled the same class of persons in modern times who find a pleasure in recording their names, or thoughts, or sentiments, in a similar manner. A favourite mode of record is that John Thomas, of London or New York, or Jaques Bonhomme, of Paris or Brussels, or of some place very far beneath the importance of those capitals, was here on a certain day. Such notices by modern travellers may be seen on the most magnificent and venerable ruins of antiquity, and even sometimes, in spite of all the care of the attendants, on the houses of Pompeii itself. The ancient perpetrator of one of these inscriptions on the walls of the basilica was little aware of the value of his labours in the eyes of posterity, when he recorded the important fact that C. Pumidius Dipilus "was here" on the 3rd of October, in the consulship of M. Lepidus and Q. Catulus. For modern investigators have hence inferred the fact that the building must be older than the year, B.C. 79, the date of that consulship, and thus probably one of the oldest round the Forum of Pompeii.

It is well known that the earliest Christian churches were built after the plan of a basilica, and some of those at Rome retain the name to this day. There were two reasons for this practice: the Christian architects naturally felt a repugnance to take the heathen temples as models, while at the same time the form of the basilica was much better adapted to the requirements of Christian worship. Such were the churches of the Lateran, the Vatican, S: Paolo fuori le Mura, Sta. Croce in Gerusalemme, Sta. Agnese, two miles beyond the Porta Pia, S. Lorenzo fuori le Mura, and SS. Petrus et Marcellinus, outside the Porta Maggiore. Some churches of a latter date also assumed the same form as those of S. Sebastian and Sta. Maria Maggiore; which latter, especially, conveys an excellent idea of the arrangement of an ancient basilica. But Sta. Agnese is the only one which has preserved the characteristic of an upper portico over a lower one.

On the northern side of the basilica, a small street, the *Strada della*

K

Marina, leads from the Forum to the Sea Gate. On the further side of this street, its main entrance facing the basilica, and its eastern side ranging along the Forum, stands the largest temple in Pompeii, commonly called the Temple of Venus. This name indeed is not better authenticated than those of the other temples in the Forum. It was at first considered to have been a Temple of Bacchus, from a couple of pictures of a Bacchic character having been found within its precincts. An inscription, wrongly interpreted, indeed, first led to the notion that it was a temple of Venus. That appellation is perhaps better supported by the consideration that as Venus was the patron goddess of Pompeii, it is reasonable to suppose that the most magnificent temple in the place was dedicated to her worship, and by the fact that in the cell was found a marble statue of Venus, something in the style of the celebrated Medicean statue at Florence, as well as a head of the same goddess. The name, however, of this, as well as of several other buildings, will never, it is to be feared, be certainly determined; unless perhaps the excavators should some day have the good fortune to discover a plan of the city like the Capitoline plan of Rome.

This temple occupies the greater part of the western side of the Forum; the length of the area in which it stands being one hundred and fifty feet, with a breadth of seventy-five feet. The court in which the temple stands is entirely surrounded by a peristyle of forty-eight columns, forming a portico between thirteen and fourteen feet in breadth. The columns, originally Doric, have been altered into Corinthian, both ill designed and executed. The lower third of them is painted yellow, and the rest is white. About two-thirds of the upper part of the oblong area in the middle is occupied by the temple. It stands, like most of the other Pompeian temples, on a lofty podium, ascended by a flight of eleven steps. It is peripteral and amphiprostyle, being surrounded with twenty-eight fluted Corinthian columns partly painted blue. The portico in front of the cell is hexatyle, or having six columns in front, with four at the sides. Within the cella, besides the statue already mentioned, was found a beautiful mosaic border, represented in the annexed cut. Before the steps leading up to the cella stood the altar. Its form, say some authorities, was not adapted for bloody or burnt sacrifices, but only for offerings of fruit, cakes, and incense—a circumstance which supports its claim to be a temple of Venus, a goddess that did not delight in bloody sacrifices. Other authorities, however, say that a piece of black stone placed upon the altar had three receptacles for fire, and that the ashes of victims were found on it. At the north end of the temple were several apartments, having an outlet to the Forum. In one destined apparently for the priest may still be

MOSAIC BORDER.

seen, though in an evanescent state, a beautiful painting of Bacchus and Silenus, carefully fastened with iron cramps and cement, showing that it had been removed by the ancients from some other place. Inside the area, on the right, is a terminal figure. The walls under the colonnade were painted in bright colours, with landscapes, country houses, and interiors with figures. There were also figures representing dancers, sacrificers to Priapus, battles with crocodiles, &c. One painting represented the dispute between Agamemnon and Achilles; another, Hector tied to the car of Achilles. Round the lower part of the wall ran a long series of dwarfish figures, of which the annexed cut will convey an idea.

DWARFS, FROM A PAINTING AT POMPEII.

In a recess under the colonnade of the Forum at the northern extremity of the wall of this temple are the public standard measures for grain, oil, and wine. Beyond the temple, and with the prison next to it, filling the remaining space of the west side of the Forum, is a long narrow quadrangular building, which is sometimes thought to have been a granary, while others have taken it for a *lesche*, or sort of coffee-house.

With the exception of the theatres and one or two more temples and

other buildings, we have now described all the public edifices of Pompeii.
There is near the theatres a small but very well preserved Temple of Isis,
one of the two whose destination is satisfactorily ascertained by an inscription found in it.   From its state of preservation, it is better calculated
perhaps than any other in Pompeii to initiate us into the mysteries of ancient
worship. A description of it, however, could not be made intelligible without
a view and a ground-plan, and we therefore pass it over.   In its neighbourhood is another small temple, or rather *sacellum*, by some called a Temple
of Jupiter and Juno, while others think that it was dedicated to Æsculapius
and Hygieia.   The statues of the divinities found in it, whoever they may
be, made of terra-cotta, are now in the national Museum at Naples.   It is
difficult to distinguish between representations of Jupiter and Æsculapius
when unaccompanied, as in the present instance, with their respective attributes.   If, however, the statues in question are those of Jupiter and Juno,
the father of gods and men sinks into insignificance beside his consort, who
is much larger than he, and quite his better half.

  Proceeding in a south-westerly direction down the street in which stands
the Temple of Isis, and which from that circumstance has been named *Strada
del Tempio d'Iside*, we come immediately after that building to another
of an oblong form having three of its sides occupied with a portico, while in
the middle of it stands a curious pediment, resembling a stone pulpit, ascended
by high steps at the back.   From some supposed connection with the adjoining temple, with which, however, there is no communication, the building in
question has been called the Curia Isiaca.   Its real destination has proved
quite a riddle to antiquarians.   From a door in it leading towards the great
theatre, it seems not improbable that it may have been in some way connected
with it.

  Beyond the Curia Isiaca, on the same side of the street, and quite at the
end of it, we come to the Propylæum forming the entrance to what has been
called the Forum Triangulare. This Propylæum has been reckoned among
the best remains of Pompeii. It consists, as will be seen in the annexed
photograph, of eight Ionic columns, raised upon two steps, which, when perfect, probably supported a kind of attic. These columns, which were about
eighteen feet in height, were made of a volcanic stone, coated with stucco and
painted yellow. Their capitals present a feature found only in monuments
of high antiquity; the volutes characteristic of the Ionic order being found
on four sides of them, instead of two joined by the usual coussinet. The

THE TRIANGULAR FORUM.

length of the façade is about fifty-four feet. Between the last two columns at the western extremity, facing the Street of the Theatres, which here
runs into the Street of Isis, stands one of those little square fountains so
often found at Pompeii. It was supplied with water through the mask
sculptured on the stone which surmounts it. A wall behind the columns, at
a distance of fourteen or fifteen feet from them, formed a spacious vestibule.
On the face of this wall may be perceived the remains of six marble consoles,
intended probably to support busts. In the vestibule were found some articles
of gold and silver and an emerald ring. The wall, as will be seen in the
view, is pierced with two gateways, one being at about the centre of it, the
other on the left at the end. On passing one of these gates we find ourselves
in a large, open, triangular space, the left hand side of which is entirely, and
the right partially, occupied by a portico consisting altogether of about a
hundred columns of the Doric order. Remains of these columns, as of those
of the Propylæum, still exist of greater or smaller height, one only being at
present entirely perfect. At the further extremity, on the edge of the hill
or plateau on which Pompeii stands, the portico is not continued. Here,
according to Mazois, there was formerly a wall built of squared stones about
thirty-six feet high; but it is now almost entirely hid by rubbish covered
with a rich vegetation, which reaches down to the road below. The longer or
eastern side of this triangular space was about four hundred and fifty feet in
length, and the other two between two hundred and fifty and three hundred.

The destination of the ample space thus enclosed has been a matter of
dispute. Some consider it to have been the Forum of ancient Pompeii,
others the Acropolis; but to the latter opinion may be objected the fact that
it lies not on the highest point of the city, the present Forum being still
higher. All that appears certain is, that, from the temple which stands in the
middle of it, and from the capability of closing the entrance, it may be inferred that it was a sacred enclosure. The interior space, which is carefully
levelled, consists at present only of earth, but may anciently have been paved
with stone or marble. To the Greek temple, which stands in the middle of
it, sometimes called the Temple of Neptune, sometimes of Hercules, we have
already adverted above. One side of the podium on which it stood is
seen in the view, on the right in the middle distance, with the altars at its
extremity. The foreground on this side shows an unexcavated portion of the
town covered with rank vegetation. In the centre of the picture, also in the
middle distance, is seen part of the great theatre. Its two upper ranges are

visible with their outer corridors opened with arcades. The entrances in the wall are upon a level with the second cavea, from which staircases ascended to that above. The large square mass of building before the theatre is thought to have been a reservoir. The modern house at a little distance behind the theatre on the left and the trees near it stand on a part of the town which has not yet been excavated. Beyond is the country through which the Sarno flows, and the background is filled by Mount St. Angelo.

Of the interior of the theatres we can give no views. They are, however, in a very tolerable state of preservation, and convey a good idea of the arrangement of such buildings in ancient times. The smaller one which adjoins the greater theatre, and with which there is a communication, is thought to have been intended for musical performances—a sort of opera-house—and with that view to have been roofed over. It would contain about fifteen hundred persons. The theatres were built on the side of a hill, so that in the great one the audience could enter on a level with the upper gallery and thus descend to their seats. It was a custom of the Greeks to select a hill side for their theatres; and this leads us to imagine that those of Pompeii were originally of Greek construction, though afterwards slightly altered to suit the customs of the Roman drama. Such a method of construction offered two advantages; it saved expense in the building, and it enabled the audience to enjoy an extensive prospect. In this last respect perhaps the Greek theatre at Taormina, between Messina and Catania in Sicily, is unrivalled. Standing nearly a thousand feet above the sea, with Ætna at its back, the view on all sides is magnificent. The ruins, too, and especially the scene, are in a very perfect state. These, however, appear to be Roman though erected on an originally Greek foundation. From the theatre at Pompeii may also be enjoyed an extensive prospect, bounded in the distance by Mount St. Angelo.

A large quadrangular enclosure behind the theatres is by some supposed to have been a barrack; by others, with more probability, a *ludus gladiatorius*, or quarters for gladiators. The frequent exhibition of gladiatorial combats at Pompeii, as appears from inscriptions, must have required a great number of gladiators to have been kept there, and the place in question would have been by no means too large for the purpose. Its destination, however, is better shown by the gladiatorial arms that have been found here, while none of the ordinary military weapons have been discovered. Among the articles found was a bronze helmet enriched with bas-reliefs, the subjects of which related to some

of the principal events of the Trojan war; also greaves for the legs highly ornamented, as represented in the annexed cuts. The masks sculptured on the
greaves represent the tragic, comic, and satiric features. The inscriptions,
too, and drawings on the walls relate to the combats of the arena.

The amphitheatre, being situated at the
south-eastern extremity of the town, and
there being no other excavations near it,
is often left unvisited by travellers; nor indeed to those who have seen any of the
Roman amphitheatres which so frequently
occur in Italy and France is there much to
attract attention in that at Pompeii. Yet

BRONZE HELMET FOUND AT POMPEII.

SPECIMEN OF THE GREAVES SUPPOSED TO HAVE
BEEN WORN BY THE GLADIATORS.

without paying it a visit our idea of the place will hardly be complete. *Seges
est ubi Troja fuit.* These vineyards which we traverse in our way to it, these
fields planted with mulberry trees and sown with lupins and corn, smile and
flourish on the surface of the fiery flood which destroyed the city. They
cover buildings as splendid perhaps as those which we have already seen,
and containing, it may be, still richer treasures of art.

The amphitheatre at Pompeii was calculated to hold about twelve thousand
persons. When we consider that at Puteoli, within twenty miles of it, there

was another, and, at a not much greater distance, the magnificent one of
Capua, we are forcibly struck with the fondness of the Roman nobles for
these bloody sports, who could not endure even in their seats of pleasure and
retirement to be deprived of them. How popular these exhibitions were is
testified, as we have already said, by the numerous *graffiti* relating to them,
as well as by the sculptures on one of the mausoleums in the Street of the
Tombs. Not only did slaves and freedmen engage in these inhuman sports,
but even persons of rank and fortune, so that Augustus found himself compelled to prohibit men of senatorial or equestrian rank from appearing as
gladiators. But some of the succeeding emperors were not so scrupulous.
Nero, who delighted in the shows of the arena, is said to have brought upon
it upwards of a thousand senators and knights; and Commodus did not hesi-
tate to disgrace the imperial purple by appearing himself numberless times

as a gladiator. The bas-reliefs
on the tomb exhibited a great
variety of these combats both
on foot and horseback, as well as
venationes, or fights with wild
beasts. We annex two or three
cuts which will convey an idea
of these combats. The first
represents an equestrian con-
test between apparently a barbarian combatant named Be-
brix, and a Roman one named Nobilior. Nobilior appears to have parried

with his buckler a thrust of Bebrix's lance,
and is about to return the blow, while Bebrix
places himself in a posture of defence. In the
second group a gladiator of the sort called a
Samnite, from the way in which he is armed,
has been conquered by another called a Myrmillo. The Samnite is holding up his left hand
to implore the mercy of the people or the emperor. If the spectators were dissatisfied with
the vanquished combatant they gave the signal
for his death by turning down their thumbs,
and his victorious antagonist was obliged to become his executioner. In the

present instance the Myrmillo seems inclined to bestow the *coup-de-grace* on his conquered adversary without waiting for the decision of the people; but he is checked by the *lanista*, or director of the combat, who seizes his sword-arm. It is remarkable that in these bas-reliefs the swords are entirely omitted, and it has been conjectured that it was intended to insert them in metal. The left arm and the upper part of the body of the combatants were always left uncovered, those parts being sufficiently protected by the shield. The third cut represents combats between the gladiators called *bestiarii* and

BESTIARII.

wild beasts. In the lower compartment a wild boar appears to be attacking a naked and defenceless man, who is in a recumbent posture, and whose only chance of safety must lie in the activity with which he avoids the onset. Beyond a wolf is running off with a javelin fixed in his breast, at which he is gnawing; while further on a stag with a rope round his horns has been pulled to the ground, in which position he is attacked by two dogs or wolves. The upper part is thought to show the manner in which the *bestiarii* were trained in their profession. Armed with a couple of javelins, the *bestiarius* is attacking a panther made fast to a bull by a collar and rope; while behind the bull another man with a lance appears to be goading him forwards. By this method the novice was in some degree secured from a sudden spring of the panther, while at the same time much more skill and wariness are required than if the panther had been fastened to an immoveable post.

We have now gone through all the public buildings of Pompeii, and must turn again to contemplate the private houses, which form indeed its most interesting features.

We need hardly observe that in Pompeii, as in other towns, ancient as well as modern, the houses varied greatly in size and splendour, from the cabins of the poorer classes to the mansions of men of equestrian and senatorial

L

rank. It is, of course, the houses of the last kind that are most calculated to attract our attention from the beauty of their architecture and the paintings and other ornaments with which they were decorated; yet it will not be uninteresting to examine a little how the middle and lower classes were lodged.

From the short notice already given of the house of Pansa, it will appear that a first-class mansion always contained two large halls or courts, called the Atrium and the Peristyle, surrounded with a number of more or less splendid rooms, serving the purposes of sleeping, eating, and drawing-rooms; while in some cases there was also a garden beyond the peristyle. The annexed photograph of the House of Cornelius Rufus, to which we have already alluded, very well displays the arrangement of the atrium, tablinum, and peristyle. Below houses of this class others descended in the following degrees: first, houses without a peristyle or a garden; second, houses without either peristyle or atrium, and containing only a few living-rooms. Yet in all the three classes there was of course often a considerable difference; the two lower degrees differing as much in size and convenience as the higher did in elegance and splendour.

A small house in the *Vicolo di Modesto*, a little way beyond that of Pansa, may serve as an example of the third class of dwellings. It has neither atrium nor peristyle; but in order to enable the family to enjoy the fresh air which the richer classes obtained in those courts, a stone bench ran along the front of the house. The street door by the side of it opened into a sort of covered hall. On the left some stairs led to an upper story, behind which there is a small apartment apparently for the slave. On the right hand side is an uncovered passage, with a well at the end of it, running along the greater part of the house; on the left of which is what appears to have been a workshop, with a door from the entrance hall, and lighted by small windows from the uncovered passage. This apartment is followed by a dining-room entered by a door from the same passage; and behind this again, quite at the further extremity of the house, a kitchen, as may be recognized by the hearth. The sleeping rooms must have been upon the upper floor.

We shall select one more house of this class, but of a much better description. It did not belong to a shopkeeper, there being no shop in it; but its owner must have been a person of small income; and as it stands close to the Gate of Herculaneum, and the steps for ascending the walls, it has been conjectured that it may have belonged to the person who had charge of the gate.

The entrance leads into a covered passage, or corridor, running along the whole side of the house; at the further end of which is a staircase leading to a small apartment, and to a terrace which extends over the length of the passage. Close to the staircase is the cell of a slave, probably the only one in the house. At the end of the passage at the foot of the stairs, a door on the left leads into what seems to have been a winter eating room. Behind this room is a kitchen, and quite in the corner of the house a small *lararium*, or domestic chapel. This place, which is a remarkable one in so small a house, had no window, and could have been lighted only by lamps. A stone bench runs round two sides of it. At the extremity of it, facing the entrance is a niche, with a painting, now almost obliterated, of Fortuna, Pomona, or some such goddess, reposing on a conch and holding a cornucopia. Before it is an altar. The greater part of the house is engrossed by a court or garden, which appears, from holes intended for that purpose, to have been covered with a trellis, and thus answered in some measure the purpose of an atrium or peristyle. It contains a stone *triclinium*, where the family during the fine weather—that is, during the greater part of the year—probably took their meals. Behind the *triclinium* is a niche for the statue of some god, to which the pious owner might make his libations; and in the corner of the court near the street door is a *puteal*, or well.

The next house that we shall instance is a middle-class one, having an atrium, or *cavædium*, but no peristyle. It is called the *Casa di Modesto*, and is situated at the bottom of the *Vicolo* of the same name near the town walls. The atrium in this case was of the kind called *displuviatum*; that is, the roof, instead of sloping down to the four sides of the square opening in the middle of it, and thus throwing the rain water into the *impluvium*, or basin below, slanted, on the contrary, away from it, towards the sides of the house, and thus threw the water outside instead of in—a very rare method of construction. The water was thus lost, which in most cases was conveyed into an underground cistern, and applied to domestic purposes. In the house in question the *impluvium* has no issue to carry the water off, being merely intended to catch the small quantity that fell through the aperture of the *compluvium*. For the same reason, not being exposed to the drippings from the roof, the *impluvium* appears to have been surrounded with a narrow flower bed. At each side of the *prothyrum*, or entrance passage, which is very long for the size of the house, were apartments. The larger one on the left was, from the stone counter in it, evidently a shop; and as it has a communication with the interior of the house, it was no doubt kept by the proprietor. The smaller rooms on the other side of the *prothyrum* served probably as a kitchen and a cell for the slave who acted as porter or door-keeper. On the further side of the atrium are two apartments handsomely decorated. Their use cannot be certainly determined, but one of them probably served as a dining-room. On the left hand side of the atrium is a flight of stairs leading to two apartments on the upper story.

Notwithstanding its small size, this house was very beautifully and taste-fully decorated with paintings, the subjects of which were taken from the Greek mythology, and from Homer's Odyssey. They have now perished; but they were perfect in 1812 when seen by Mazois, who took copies of them. One of them represented Ulysses drawing his sword upon Circe to avenge his companions transformed by the enchantress. Circe is using the suppli-catory gesture so frequently described in the Greek poets, by falling on her knees and endeavouring to clasp with one hand the knee of Ulysses, while she stretches out the other to touch his beard. Her head is surrounded with a *nimbus*, or glory, which appears like a plate of solid gold, resembling that seen round the heads of saints in early Christian pictures. Another painting represented Ulysses discovering Achilles at Scyros among the daughters of Lycomedes.

What we have here said will suffice to convey a general idea of the in-ferior classes of houses. We have already described the general arrange-ment of a first class house when speaking of that of Pansa (above, p. 43); but we shall here add a few more particulars.

The fronts even of the best houses were in general very plain, the taste and money of the proprietor being employed in decorating the interior. It has been already observed that, with the exception of the suburban villa of Diomedes, there is not a house in the place that possesses anything like a front portico. The house of Diadumenus, not far from the Stabian Baths, excavated in the present year, has perhaps the most aristocratic kind of ap-proach, as the pavement in front of it is raised some feet above the level of the street, and must be ascended by steps at each end. The street door, which was lofty and narrow, was commonly decorated on each side with pilasters, as shown in the cut already given of the entrance to the house of Pansa (above, p. 42). These pilasters are seldom of any regular order, and are frequently fantastically decorated. Often on the threshold some inscrip-tion in mosaic, such as *Salve*, or *Have* (*Ave* with the aspirate), bids the visitor welcome, and bespeaks, as it were, beforehand the hospitality of the owner. Some of the devices met with, however, are not of so inviting a character. Thus in that of the Tragic Poet, the first thing which meets the eye of the visitor on entering is a large fierce dog, executed in mosaic, in the act apparently of springing upon him, though he is secured with a collar and chain. The animal is well executed; he is black, spotted with white, and the collar is red. Beneath is written in large letters *Cave Canem*, " Beware the dog."

This mosaic has been removed to the entrance of one of the rooms in the National Museum. In some cases a bear, dolphin, or other animal is represented; in others some emblem, as an anchor or a rudder, which may typify, perhaps, the profession of the owner.

On passing the prothyrum and entering the atrium of a first class house, the *coup-d'œil* is very striking; and without examining whether all the details are in the best taste, it must of course have been more so when everything was

MOSAIC AT THE ENTRANCE OF THE PROTHYRUM OF THE TRAGIC POETS' HOUSE.

in a perfect state. The large array of columns that meets the eye, the fountains that played in the middle of those extensive courts are calculated to impress the modern visitor with the idea that he is entering a public building rather than a private residence. Hence the most splendid and luxurious modern capitals, such as London or Paris, if buried to-morrow by a volcanic eruption from Primrose Hill or Montmartre, would not—setting aside their public buildings—convey the idea of so much magnificence as this small provincial town. The difference is to be explained by the different habits of ancient and modern life, and the different building arrangements which were in consequence adopted. The ancient Romans, from their republican habits, which being once fixed were not easily changed under the empire, lived more in public than we do. A man of the higher class had not only to receive and entertain his acquaintance and private friends, but also a large number of clients and retainers. These last came only, as to a levee, to consult the great man and pay their respects; they did not perhaps sleep at his house, or even dine with him, but they would require an ample space for their reception. Hence, while a modern house is principally occupied with rooms for the accommodation of the family, these in an ancient one were curtailed to the smallest possible dimensions. These different purposes required a different arrangement in the whole plan of the house. The ancient house occupied a larger area than the modern one. It was more spread out, and did not rise into several stories, having commonly only one above the ground floor. We are speaking of course only of the houses of Pompeii. At Rome, where the ground was more valuable, they often rose to the height of six or seven stories; and Augustus was obliged to check the tendency this way by prohibiting the building of houses more than seventy feet high. Such houses as those of Pansa or the Faun, in an area of two hundred feet (without the garden) by one hundred, contained perhaps fifty different apartments of one kind or another, while a modern architect perhaps would not put more than a quarter of the number into the same space. The greater part of them indeed are little better than closets, the atrium and the peristyle occupying the chief portion of the area. It was the former of these that was devoted to public purposes, while the peristyle and surrounding apartments were for the private use of the family.

It is often said that these Pompeian houses must have been very uncomfortable dwellings. Viewed through the medium of our northern habits they may be so; but comfort is a relative term, and in such cases depends very much upon climate and habits of life. In the warm sunny weather, which in southern Italy prevails during the greater part of the year, that open, airy, cheerful space, rendered still more refreshing by the sight and sound of water thrown from the fountains, and by the aspect and fragrance of beds of the choicest flowers, must have been in the highest degree delightful. Those spacious, shady porticoes formed an in-door promenade, sheltered both from rain and sun, and might even serve for a sort of supplementary apartments. To be shut up during a few wintry days in small rooms, yet on that account all the more capable of being easily warmed, was a small price to pay for such enjoyments.

The aspect of the interior of a first-class house is well conveyed by the photographic view already given of that of Cornelius Rufus (see above, p. 74), and will be further illustrated by that annexed, representing the

HOUSE OF HOLCONIUS.

peristyle of the house of Hólconius. This house is among the more recent excavations, having been finally cleared in 1861, though some of the shops at its sides were discovered at a very early period. It stands at the corner of the Street of the Holconii and that of the Theatres, its principal entrance being in the former.

As we can give no ground-plan of the house, it would be wearisome to enter into a detail of all its parts, and we shall therefore confine ourselves to those adjacent to the peristyle. The tablinum stood just in front of the columns seen in the foreground of the view. It affords a normal example of that apartment, being entirely open towards the atrium, but capable of being shut on the side towards the peristyle by sliding doors of wood, of the jambs of which remains may still be seen fixed to the wall with iron cramps. The floor was of pounded brick incrusted with small pieces of marble, while the walls were adorned with paintings now almost destroyed. Among them may be recognized a representation of the story of Luna and Endymion, and Leda with a nest full of children. Near the tablinum was found a skeleton, supposed to be that of the lady of the house, who seems to have been endeavouring to make her escape with her treasures, but was here overwhelmed and prostrated in death. She had with her a box containing her valuables; among which the most remarkable is a necklace composed of various amulets. She had also with her several small locks. Three more skeletons were found in different parts of the building. There were also discovered small glass bottles for perfumes, and essences, and other articles.

Before the tablinum stood two detached columns as shown in the view. The remainder of the colonnade of the peristyle surrounded a *xystus*, or flower garden, in the middle of which is a small square *piscina*, or basin, between six and seven feet deep. In the centre is a pillar supporting a round marble table, from the middle of which rose a *jet-d'eau*. On the further side of the garden is another fountain, consisting of a boy, sculptured in white marble, standing on a pedestal, having under one arm a goose, whilst, from a vase held in the other, the water flowed down a little staircase in front of the pedestal. Water also spirted from pipes in several of the columns at a height of about four feet from the ground, falling into a tolerably broad channel, or gutter, which ran round the garden. Thus was presented quite a little system of waterworks, which in warm weather, combined with the colours and scent of the flowers, must have had a delightfully refreshing effect. In the walls of the *piscina*, are eight iron hooks, meant apparently to keep fish, fruit, or other articles cool in the water, which, from its continual motion, was always fresh. In front of the *piscina* is seen another round marble table.

Over the roof of the portico, supported by the pillars, ran a gallery, with another set of columns, ascended by a staircase near the tablinum. This gallery gave access to the apartments on the upper floor. The peristyle is simply decorated. The lower third of the columns, having the channelling only marked with lines, is painted red, while the upper and channelled part is white. The walls are black, and adorned with small pictures of eatables, separated by ornaments. The border at the bottom is painted with water-plants and water fowl. On the wall on the right was a *graffito*, to the following effect: "July 7th, lard 200lb, garlic 250 bundles;" meaning probably that these things were either bought or sold on that day.

Two of the rooms on the further side of the peristyle, and at the extremity of the house, are visible in the view. The smaller one on the right appears to be a bed-chamber. The floor is of *opus Signinum;* the walls, painted mostly red and yellow, besides the architectural ornaments so commonly met with, have pictures of Nereids riding through the waves on sea-monsters. The picture facing the entrance, so far as can be made out, represents the Dioscuri. Next to this apartment, on the left, is a large and handsome *exedra*, or retiring room. It is paved with black and white marble, and has in the middle a small *impluvium*, or basin; from which we may infer that there was a corresponding aperture in the roof. The walls were adorned with small but well-executed pictures. One in the front represents Narcissus admiring himself in the fountain. That on the left wall has for its subject a Hermaphrodite leaning on the shoulder of Silenus; that on the right, Bacchus accompanied by his thiasos, that is, his usual troop, or rout, discovering Ariadne.

This last subject is a very common one in the paintings at Pompeii; but as it is well treated in this instance, and as the picture is in a very tolerable state of preservation, we have inserted a photograph of it.

Bacchus, after his arrival in Naxos, finds Ariadne sunk in a profound slumber. Her face is hid in the pillows; over her head stands Sleep, with outspread wings, as if to take his departure, and bearing in his left hand a torch reversed, a symbol common to him with his brother Death. A young Faun lifts the sheet, or veil, in which Ariadne is enveloped, in an attitude expressive of surprise at her beauty, and looks earnestly at the god,

FRESCO OF BACCHUS AND ARIADNE.

as if to discover what impression it makes upon him. Bacchus, crowned with ivy and berries, clothed in a short tunic and flowing pallium, having on his legs rich buskins, and holding in his right hand the thyrsus bound with a fillet, appears to be approaching slowly and cautiously, for fear that he should awake the nymph. Meanwhile, a Bacchante in the back-ground raises her tambourine, and seems to strike it strongly, as if summoning the Bacchic troop to descend from the mountains. At the head of them is Silenus, also crowned with ivy, and supporting his footsteps with a long knotted staff. He is followed by a Faun playing on the double flute, and by eight Bacchantes. On a part of the mountain to the left, from which springs a tree, another Bacchante and Faun are looking on the scene below.*
Around the picture is painted a sort of frame.

The general appearance of a wall decorated with paintings in this style will be better understood by a view of one in the house of Siricus, or Salve Lucrum. This house, excavated in 1851, adjoins the Stabian Baths, in the *Vico del Lupanare*, but has its principal entrance in the *Strada Stabiana*; from an inscription near which it derives its first name. Its second name was taken from a mosaic inscription on the threshold of the atrium, *Salve lucru*, with the customary omission of the *m*; meaning, "Welcome, gain!" from which it has been inferred that the owner was engaged in trade. The house is a sort of double one, being connected with that called the House of the Russian Princes. It is chiefly remarkable for its paintings, which are in a good state of preservation. The best of them are three in the apartment called the Exedra. The first of these represents Neptune and Apollo presiding over the building of the walls of Troy; the second, Thetis presenting herself to Vulcan to demand the arms of Achilles; and in the third, which is that seen to the left in our view, is depicted the drunken Hercules. The figures are about one third of the natural size.

The demi-god has been sacrificing to Bacchus, whose altar is seen in the middle of the picture, and has only been too pious in his devotions. Crowned with ivy, clothed in a short, red, transparent tunic, Hercules, overcome with wine, has fallen on the ground, at the foot of a tree, and with difficulty supports himself with his left arm; the right is elevated in the air, and he seems endeavouring to snap his fingers, to express, with the characteristic *abandon* of drunkenness, the nothingness of all human affairs in

* Fiorelli, "Giornale degli Scavi," No. iii. p. 87.

M

comparison of jollity, good eating, and particularly good drinking. Behind him a little cupid is carrying off his cup. On the altar, which is bedecked with garlands, three cupids, assisted by a fourth, who has climbed the tree, are elevating on their shoulders the hero's quiver; while four others on the ground, to the left of the altar, are trying to raise his ponderous club. This part of the picture has often been expressed on gems. At the base of the altar is a votive tablet, with the image of Bacchus, declaring the deity to whom it was sacred.

On the left of the picture, in an elevated position, is a beautiful group of three females, scantily clothed, and having on their wrists refulgent bracelets. She, in the middle, who sits on a rock, with a fan in her hand, a customary attribute of Venus, is probably Omphale, with her Lydian handmaids, who seem to look with complacency on the hero's condition, as tending to rivet his servitude. A little grove, and a column with a vase upon it, terminate the view on this side.

On a mountain top, probably that of Tmolus, on the right of the picture, Bacchus, accompanied by Fauns and Bacchantes, is gazing intently on the son of Alcmena. His attitude is one of tranquil repose and satisfaction, as he appears to converse with his followers. A Bacchante leans over the god; the raised arm of a Faun on the left expresses his joy and admiration at the scene; another, on the right, manifests the same feelings by removing his pan-pipe from his lips, and breaking off the tune that he was playing.

This picture, for the grace and harmony of its composition, as well as its freshness of colouring and delicacy of handling, is one of the most important monuments of the pictorial art discovered at Pompeii. Two of the groups, that of Hercules, and that of Omphale, are found repeated in separate pictures; but this is the only instance yet discovered in which the three groups are combined together, and form one picture: nor is that of Bacchus and his companions to be found elsewhere. The whole is thought to refer to a satyric drama on the subject of the Lydian Hercules.

The spacious and lofty *exedra* in which these paintings are has a threshold of white mosaic, bordered with black zones, with ornaments in the middle like shields, in the shape of a half moon. The floor is painted with black fillets, except a piece of mosaic in the centre, in which are represented two *diota*, or double-handled wine jars, with shoots of vine which interlace and surround a rectangular piece of marble, formed of twenty-two squares of *giallo antico*. The walls, which are painted in yellow compartments on a

FRESCO IN HOUSE OF SIRICUS.

red ground, terminate above in a bold scroll border, within the spirals of which are depicted quadrupeds and winged Cupids in various attitudes. Above this border, up to the roof, the walls are painted with pieces of architecture and other ornaments. The whole is surmounted by a small cornice supporting the roof, which is richly decorated with stuccos and gilt bas-reliefs. The three pictures before mentioned are upon a red ground, and framed as it were in a meander, in the fashion of a cornice, and adorned at the corners with fantastically shaped animals. At the sides of them are seen capricious pieces of architecture, on the top of which, as on an acroterium, stand centaurs and beasts in ferocious attitudes. Those on each side of the picture of Hercules contain the image of Apollo Musagetes, with the bow and lyre (not seen in the photograph), and the Muse Calliope, with a roll of paper in her hand. The remaining Muses, painted on a yellow ground, with accurate execution and vivid colouring, decorate the other compartments of the *exedra*, together with some views of houses and landscapes. The *podium*, or part near the floor, is painted black and divided into square compartments, ornamented with festoons of plants attached to candelabra supporting spheres, with aquatic plants, *bucrania*, or ox heads, and Bacchic vases.*

The house of Holconius contains several well-preserved pictures, besides that of Bacchus and Ariadne already described; but which, as we can give no copies of them, need not here detain us.

Another handsome house, with well-preserved pictures, but of very unequal merit, is that of Marcus Lucretius, in the *Strada Stabiana*, called at first the *Casa delle Suonatrici*, or House of the Female Musicians, from paintings found in it. We have before remarked that this is one of the only two houses in Pompeii of which the names of the owners are satis-

factorily ascertained; in the present case, by means of a painting containing a letter addressed, M. LUCRETIO FLAM. MARTIS DECURI- ONI POMPEI(IO); or, "to M. Lu- cretius, Priest of Mars and De- curion of Pompeii." We annex a woodcut of this device. Lucre- tius, therefore, must have been a

ADDRESS OF LUCRETIUS.

* See Fiorelli, "Giornale degli Scavi," No. xiii. p. 12, sqq.

man of much consideration in the town. His house is a large one, but irregular in its plan. It seems to have been under repair at the time of the eruption; at least, we cannot in any other way account for the rough state in which the *impluvium*, or water-basin, in the atrium was found. It was no doubt intended to be lined with marble; in its present state it forms a strong contrast with the elegance of the rest of the atrium. This has a pavement of white mosaic; the lower part of the walls is painted in imitation of variously-coloured marbles; above, they are blue and ornamented with grotesques; the whole surmounted by a frieze of gilt stucco, many fragments of which were found during the excavation. A *lararium*, or shrine of the Lares, stands on the right on entering. It is not, however, so handsome as the *lararium* in the house of Diadumenus, excavated this year. The bed-chambers, and other rooms which surround the atrium, contained several good pictures, some of which have been removed to the Museum at Naples.

The most notable thing in the house, however, is the fountain in the peristyle, of which a view is given in the accompanying photograph. This view also shows the tablinum, or apartment which usually intervenes between the atrium and the peristyle. It is raised, in this case, as will be seen, one step above the pavement of the atrium. Its floor consists of a white marble mosaic, surrounded with narrow black borders. In the middle is a slab of *giallo antico*, encircled with a border of variegated mosaic. The walls are richly decorated with pieces of architecture, and in the middle of them are spaces for two large pictures, which must have been removed before the eruption. The wooden frames in which the pictures were contained have left their impressions on the stucco, as well as the marks of two horizontal supports at the back of them. These marks, which are about two inches deep, have led some writers to suppose that the pictures were painted on wood. Whether, however, there were any such at Pompeii is a moot point; and Overbeck contends that the supports at the back might have served as well for a thin stucco tablet as to bind together the pieces of a wooden one. The ceiling of the tablinum was also of stucco, with coloured panels and gilt rosettes in the centre of them, as appears from numerous fragments which were discovered.

The level of the peristyle is about three feet higher than that of the tablinum, as shown by the dwarf wall on the further side of the apartment; a circumstance which brings the small figures composing the fountain more

HOUSE OF LUCRETIUS.

under the view of the spectator. In order to enter the peristyle, the visitor must ascend a flight of seven steps in the *fauces*, or narrow passage, on the left of the tablinum. On these steps was found a skeleton. The peristyle is small for so good a house; the atrium, on the contrary, is proportionately large, and there is a second atrium quite at the extremity of the house on the left, with another entrance in a little by-street. The peristyle is surrounded on two of its sides with square columns, painted with plants on a red ground. The pillars are connected together by a low wall, which leaves two openings into the *xystus*, or garden. On the other sides it is bounded by the tablinum in front, and by an *exedra*, or *œcus*, on the right. On the left, two small apartments look upon it, in one of which, apparently a library or study, was found the painting before mentioned, with the name of Lucretius.

The interior of the peristyle, instead of having a *viridarium*, or flower bed, is entirely occupied with the singular fountain, or system of fountains, seen in the view. On the further side is a small vaulted alcove, approached by five steps, and decorated with mosaics, shell-work, and painting. It contains a small marble figure of Silenus. His hair, beard, and the hide with which he is partly covered, bear traces of having been painted red. On his left is a small pillar supporting a sort of leather bottle, painted black, on which he leans, and from which the water issued. At the bottom of the steps it was collected into a square stone trough, or channel, which conducted it into a circular basin in the middle of the court. This basin, which is between six and seven feet in diameter, and rather more than two feet deep, has in its centre a hollow column, covered with *giallo antico*, whence sprung a *jet-d'eau*. On each side of the steps of the principal fountain are two Hermæ with double heads. One of these represents Bacchus and Ariadne, the other a Faun and Bacchante. There are two similar Hermæ in the foreground, near the tablinum, each representing a bearded Bacchus and a Bacchante. Near these are two singular sculptures of Cupids riding on dolphins, and entwined by polypuses. In the middle is a small group, of very middling execution, representing a young Faun extracting a thorn from the foot of a Satyr. The larger sculptures on the left are of a much better description. The further one represents a Faun with his hand raised over his head as if to protect it from the sun's rays. Before him is the figure of a Satyr, terminating below in a Hermes. He holds in his right hand a syrinx, or pan-pipe, and under his left arm a little kid, whilst a she-goat raises herself to his legs, as if asking back her young. The basin is surrounded with figures of animals of various sizes, among which may be distinguished a duck, two cows reposing, two ibises, &c. These pieces of sculpture have nothing in common with one another, and are so preposterously assorted as not to give us any very high idea of the taste of M. Lucretius. His house terminates the excavations towards the east, as will be perceived by the trees and earth in the back-ground.

The idea of a fountain in mosaic has been carried out in several places on a larger scale than here. Two houses in the Street of Mercury, called from this feature the House of the Great Fountain and the House of the Little Fountain, were discovered at an early period of the excavations. Another of the same kind was excavated in 1865, in a house in the Street of the Augustals, nearly opposite to that known as the House of the Rudder and Trident. This fountain, which stands in a garden behind the tablinum, is ornamented with mosaic and shell-work, and represents in its middle compartment Neptune standing in the sea, surrounded with all sorts of fishes. The topmost compartment seems to represent a recumbent nymph or Nereid. At the sides are Cupids and masks, and the whole is surmounted with a cornice and pediment. We annex a photograph.

It is natural to inquire how these houses, of which we see only the bare walls, were furnished; but, unfortunately, it is a question which cannot be very satisfactorily answered. The greater part of the furniture, being made of wood, has vanished, and it is chiefly from paintings that we must be content to derive our knowledge of it. On the whole, perhaps, we may conclude that it was not so elaborate in its nature as our own. The extensive area occupied by open courts, and the comparative smallness of the habitable rooms, did not render much furniture necessary. The marble or mosaic floors, and the painted stucco walls, required no carpets or paper-hangings. The beds seem often to have stood in alcoves or recesses in the walls, and there are indications that they were protected by a pole and rings with curtains. Traces of a folding screen have also been found, which may have served the same purpose. The painting of a bed in the small house near the Gate of Herculaneum, already described, shows one closely resembling a modern French bed. The bedstead seems to be either gold, or gilt wood or metal. The mattress is white, with violet stripes and gold star-like spots. The cushion was also violet. We annex a woodcut of this piece of furniture. It was probably in this instance more richly decorated

36ᵃ

MOSAIC FOUNTAIN.

than usual, since it served, as already intimated, for the couch of some god-

dess; but beds of the same form
were probably in common use. They
were made of wood, bronze, and
sometimes of ivory; and, as may be
imagined, varied very much in the
style and richness of their decoration. The bedstead, however, was
often nothing more than a sort of
bulk, constructed of brick or stone,
seven or eight foot long, three broad,

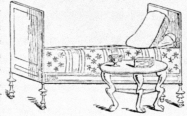

BED AND TABLE, FROM A PAINTING.

and only about two to two and a-half high, on which the mattress and
cushions were laid.

The triclinium, or couch, which surrounded three sides of the dining
table, was also sometimes made of stone, as we have already seen in the
instances of the funeral triclinium in the Street of the Tombs, and in the
house just mentioned at the Herculaneum Gate. In the dining-rooms of
the better houses, however, and especially those destined for winter use,
they seem to have been of wood, as we do not often find in them remains
of stone or brick benches. A dining apartment in the house of Lucretius,
before described, to the right of the tablinum, contained vestiges of such

a couch. It appears to have been a handsome piece of furniture from the remains of
it, consisting of its eight feet of carved wood,
fastened to the floor by an iron spike in the
centre, and covered with wrought silver, to
which no doubt they owe their preservation.
On these triclinia, when in use, was spread
a sort of mattress, with bolsters or pillows,
on which the guest leant with his left arm,
leaving the right free, to help himself from
the table.

Of chairs and stools there are more remains, and they are also found more frequently depicted in paintings. The com-
monest form is a folding stool without arms
or back, its legs usually representing those of

CURULE CHAIR, FROM A PICTURE IN POMPEII.

some animal, and the seat being composed of cloth or leather stretched over girths. Such stools were sometimes made of bronze. There were also chairs with backs, rounded so as to make a very comfortable seat. The arm chair, *solium*, or throne, with a high strait back, was the chair of the gods, or distinguished persons. In p. 87 is a cut of a curule chair, from a picture. Of the bisellium, or seat of honour, used in the theatres or at other public spectacles by those to whom it has been granted, we have already spoken.

Examples of tables are rarer than those of chairs, nor do the ancients appear to have possessed such a variety of them as we; but they seem sometimes to have been adorned with almost fabulous luxury. Their dining tables were of different sorts, sometimes having one foot, sometimes several; but the tripod is the most usual form of ancient table. The dining apparatus seems sometimes to have consisted of a stone table with one foot, on which was placed a moveable frame or tray (*ferculum*) containing the dishes. The tray was changed according to the number of courses. Marble tables,

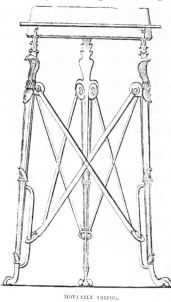

MOVEABLE TRIPOD.

with beautifully sculptured legs, were perhaps sometimes used as dining tables, but more usually for the display of some rich and costly article, as a vase, a lamp, a small statue, or the like. Such tables were commonly placed in the tablinum, though in a somewhat different form they are also found in the atrium, and most commonly over a well behind the *impluvium*, where they might serve to hold drinking vessels, or things intended to be cooled in the water. There is an elegant specimen of such a table in the atrium of the house of Cornelius Rufus, a view of which has been given above (p. 74). In this instance, as will be seen, the table is wanting, and the legs alone remain, sculptured in the resemblance of some fabulous animal, and joined together by a marble slab, also richly sculptured. They had also small bronze tables, gene-

rally tripods, very elegantly wrought, which served, like the small tables in
our drawing-rooms, to hold a vase of flowers, or any similar purpose. Some
times these had a top of *rosso antico*, or some other costly marble. Such
tables were frequently constructed to open or shut at pleasure, each of the
legs being united to the others by two braces, the lower ends of which moved
up and down upon rings, while at the upper ends, and where they crossed
each other, they could only move round a pin or hinge. The construction of this kind of table is shown in the cut in p. 88; which, however, is a
very plain specimen of such a piece of furniture.

Of all the articles of ancient domestic use, lamps and candelabra are
those which have come down to us in the greatest number and variety.
The Roman lamp, so far as its use was concerned, was of the most simple
and primitive description. They had none of our contrivances for concen-
trating the flame by means of a glass, &c. The ancient lamp consisted of a
round and usually flat vessel to contain the oil and the wick, which last projected from a hole made for it, something after the fashion of the common
lamps still used in cellars. The wick consisted merely of a few threads of
twisted flax drawn through this hole in the upper surface. A single specimen of an ancient wick has been accidentally preserved. It consists of
combed but not spun flax, twisted into a sort of string. It owes its preservation to its contact with the metal; a circumstance which has also preserved some other easily perishable materials: as, for instance, linen purses,
the linings of bronze helmets, &c. (Overbeck, ii. 56). There was nothing to
steady its flame, or to prevent its being agitated by every breeze; and the
usual way to increase the light was to increase the number of lamps. Hence
the astonishing quantity of them discovered at Pompeii, about five hundred
of them having been found in one of the corridors alone of the old Baths,
and upwards of a thousand in the entire building. Lamps of this common
sort were made of baked clay; but those of a handsomer description were
of bronze, and sometimes even of gold. The varying and tasteful forms of
the more expensive kind of lamps, and the beauty and elegance of their
workmanship, form a striking contrast with their clumsiness of construction
as articles of use; and while they betray the superiority of ancient taste over
modern, illustrate at the same time the more practical genius of the present
times.

The ancients, however, had a contrivance for increasing the light thrown
by one lamp, by multiplying the number of the wick-holes. Thus there are

lamps for one wick, for two or three wicks, and up to as many as a dozen or fourteen. In order to elevate the lamp, so that it might throw its light further than if it stood upon the bare table, bronze stands were used, often of very elegant workmanship. We give an example in the annexed cut of

one of these stands, supporting a bronze lamp for two wicks, adorned with great taste, and having upon its cover the device of a little boy wrestling with a goose, one of the prettiest designs of ancient plastic art. For atria and public buildings, where the lamp was to stand alone, tall and slender candelabra were used, having at the top a disc or plinth to hold the lamp. The richer sorts of these candelabra are decorated with a profusion of ornaments, and some are beautifully damasked or inlaid with other metals. Sometimes the shaft represents

BRONZE LAMP AND STAND.

a slender channelled column, sometimes a tree throwing out shoots or buds. As a rule they stand on three feet, representing the claws of some animal, as a lion or griffin. In some cases, instead of a plinth, the lamps were hung by chains from projections on the top of the shaft, as if from the boughs of a tree. Some of them have a sliding shaft, resembling that of a music stand, so that the light may be raised or lowered at pleasure.

Great numbers of terra-cotta vases have also been found, of which that represented in the annexed woodcut is a favourable specimen. The lip and the base have an ovolo moulding. The handles are formed apparently of interlaced branches, terminating in the heads of animals. The neck is black, with the same device, painted in white on each side, of a chariot drawn either by four panthers or tigers at full speed. A winged genius holds the reins in his left hand, and goads the animals with a javelin which he brandishes in his right. Before the quadriga is another winged figure with a thyrsus in

TERRA-COTTA VASE.

his left hand, whilst with the right he appears to be seizing the reins. A few of the details in this design are painted yellow, while the car and the mantle of the genius are red.

We will just advert to a few articles for a lady's toilette. The annexed cut represents two mirrors, one square, the other round. For these, steel was the usual material, though occasionally they are made of glass. Above them is a lighted lamp with two wicks; and on the table by their side a box of pins. The latter article, as appears from a passage in Pliny, was manufactured at Sidon. The next cut exhibits a few articles of jewellery, drawn of the same size as the originals. No. 1 is a front and side view of an ear-ring, consisting of a thick plain gold spheroid, having a metal hook at the back to fasten it to the ear. No. 2 is an ear-ring of simpler construction, with pearl pendents. No. 3 is a breast-pin, consist-

MIRRORS, &c.

ing of a Bacchanalian figure with the wings of a bat, typifying the drowsiness which follows long potations. Belts of grapes are twined across his body, and in one hand he holds a patera, in the other a glass. The fourth article is a ring with serpents' heads, a sufficiently common device.

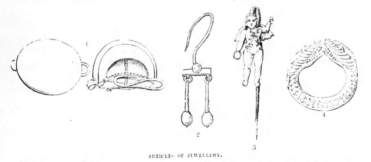

ARTICLES OF JEWELLERY.

From the drawing-room and the bedchamber we will descend for a moment into the kitchen, where, however, we shall not find much to arrest our attention. The want of a fire-place appears to have been in a good measure supplied by braziers, which served to warm the rooms, to keep dishes hot, to boil water, and perhaps to perform some minor culinary operations. The sides of these machines were hollow, to contain water, the centre was filled with lighted charcoal, which, by means of a trivet above it, might perform the operations of boiling, stewing, or frying. We annex a cut of one of these machines of a more ornamental character than usual. It is fourteen

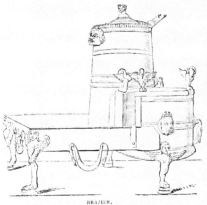

inches square, exclusive of a semicircular projection raised above the rim of the brazier, and hollowed to receive water. On the top of it are three eagles, their heads curved downwards towards their breasts, and intended apparently to support a boiler. At the side of this semicircular part rises a sort of tower with a moveable lid, having a bust for its handle. The water was drawn off through a mask in front of the machine. The ancient pots and cauldrons do not differ so much from our

BRAZIER.

own as to require any particular description; but it may be observed that they are generally more elegant in their forms. The annexed cut represents

a cooking vessel on a tripod, with a frying-pan on each side, not much differing in form from our own.

We will close this brief sketch of Pompeii with some account of its art, and especially its paintings; for which we must acknowledge our obligations to a chapter in the second volume of Overbeck's work. The pictorial remains of Hercula-

COOKING UTENSILS.

neum and Pompeii—and fortunately in the latter town they are very numerous—cannot be too highly prized; for while there are ample remains of ancient sculpture and ancient architecture, these are almost the only specimens from which we can form any idea of the art of painting in antiquity. But before entering upon an examination of them, we will say a few words on the technical methods in which they were executed.

The ancients appear to have painted, by means of different processes, on wood, cloth, parchment, ivory, and plaster; but for our present purpose it will suffice to divide their paintings into two classes—easel pictures and wall pictures, or frescoes. Of these two kinds, specimens of the latter only are preserved at Pompeii. That easel pictures were painted there we know from representations of artists employed upon them; and that finished pictures were sometimes let into the walls is also certain from unequivocal traces; nevertheless it is doubtful whether any pictures so let in were on wood; and at all events, if they were, none such have been preserved; for all the pictures which appear to have been so inserted are certainly on stucco. There is no Pompeian easel picture now in existence, and we must therefore confine ourselves to the examination of the frescoes.

Many researches have been made into the mode in which these pictures were executed; the method of preparing the ground for them, the nature of the colours used, and the manner of laying them on have been minutely examined. These researches have been aided by chemical analyses of half-destroyed pictures and of raw colours found in shops; but, though much has been learnt in this way, these researches have not served to clear up every doubt, and to establish one single and incontestable theory. Chemical analysis has shown that the colours are almost exclusively derived from the animal kingdom. Of vegetable colours there is but coal-black; and of animal colours only two, and those very seldom used; a purple made of the secretion of the purple snake mixed with chalk (*purpurissum*) and ivory black. The pure colours, through the mixing of which the different shades and tones were produced, were: for white, white chalk—not *cerussa*, or white lead, though that was also sometimes used; for yellow, ochre (*sil*), mixed with chalk to make different shades, and with red lead to produce an orange; for red, red earth or chalk, red lead (*minium*), burnt ochre, and, more seldom, cinnabar; for blue, oxide of copper; for brown, burnt ochre; which, however, like green, is usually found as a mixed colour.

To prepare the wall for painting on, it was first spread rough-cast with a thick coat of lime mixed with pozzolana; over which was laid one or several coats of fine lime-mortar; and over this again two, or, when very carefully prepared, three coats of very fine mortar, very finely powdered plaster, or powdered marble being applied to the surface of each layer. Each of these coats was laid on before that immediately preceding it had become quite dry. The second and the last coat were beaten down and smoothed with a *baculus,* or sort of strickle, and thus was produced the admirable firmness and smoothness of grounds prepared in this manner. The surface thus obtained never cracked, and was of so firm a substance that it could be sawn off like a piece of marble, and so fixed in another wall: a process not only anciently employed at Pompeii, but also since its rediscovery, in order to convey the pictures painted on this substance to the museum.

It was formerly a very general opinion that the pictures painted on the surfaces thus prepared were painted *a fresco* on the still moist stucco. In accordance with this view the pictures were no sooner discovered than they were immediately daubed with a preservative varnish, thus rendering all chemical experiments impossible. More recent experiments have been variously estimated, and there is still a great difference of opinion as to the mode in which the wall-paintings were executed. Some writers hold that *fresco* was the usual method, others decide for painting *a tempera* on the dry stucco, while some assume a mixed method, like O. Müller, who, in his " Archæologie der Kunst" (§ 319, 5), asserts that at Herculaneum the ground colours are painted *a fresco,* the rest *a tempera ;* and if it be true that this method was pursued at Herculaneum, it might also have obtained at Pompeii. Other writers have decided for an encaustic method ; and that encaustic was used at Pompeii is incontestable, as colours prepared with resin were found in a shop there, while one of the pictures in the Pantheon seems to be an allegorical representation of the art. In this method the colours were prepared with wax or resin, and rendered fluid by the admixture of some ethereal oil ; they were then laid on with a brush, and melted into the ground with a hot iron, and at the same time spread and toned down. This method, however, seems rather to have been applied to easel pictures on wood, to the painting of architectural members in stone ; perhaps also of statues and bas-reliefs. For as by this method the colours remained uninjured by the weather, it was well adapted for all sorts of out-of-door work. It may possibly also have been now and then applied to wall-painting ; but that it was universally so applied may be unequivocally denied.

Overbeck, from his own private researches, is of opinion that three distinct methods may be traced. The first of these is pure fresco. Walls which were to serve as grounds for some other technical method were universally prepared in this way ; also all imitations of marble and other stones, as well as architectural paintings. Perhaps also a few of the larger pictures in the middle of walls are in fresco; but, as a rule, these are done in one of the two methods which we shall now proceed to describe.

Both these methods differ from fresco in the circumstance that the colouring may be scraped off or removed without damaging the ground; while they differ from each other as follows:—

In the first of them the colours are very thickly laid on, but run off thin towards the edges, holding fast to the ground, and fastest where they are thinnest. Although they can be scraped off they cannot be removed with a sharp blade. In this way are executed ornaments, fantastic pieces of architecture, plants, flowers, animals, most of the small landscapes, and the flying figures on the walls. These objects are painted on walls which have been already coloured *a fresco*, the ground of which, when they are removed, appears uninjured. Yet, when such designs are subjected to chemical analysis, they do not show a trace of lime or any other organic binding medium, so that we are quite in the dark as to the nature of them.

The most singular method is the second kind of *tempera*, the characteristics of which are that the body of colour is thinner but more evenly laid on throughout. It cannot be easily scratched off, but may be removed with a knife in larger or smaller patches of the thickness of a card, when the ground below, whether it has been painted or not, remains uninjured. It is in this way that most of the large pictures are executed, as well as many of the flying figures; but in no case do we find the mere ornaments and smaller objects thus painted. From some chemical tests, not, however, very extensively applied, Overbeck could discover no traces of resin or white of eggs: he thinks, however, that lime was present in such pictures, but in very small quantities; a circumstance which may perhaps be accounted for by the lapse of eighteen centuries.

The style of painting in the Pompeian pictures is bold and free, and consequently sometimes hasty and careless. The outline seems to have been drawn with chalk or charcoal, and sometimes to have been scratched with a sharp point. In some cases, especially in landscapes, it may be doubted whether there was any outline at all, so that, when closely examined, the boundaries cannot be distinguished. The upper parts of pictures, not being so well seen, are more carelessly treated than the lower parts. It may readily be supposed that different hands were employed upon the same wall; the large pictures being undertaken by a superior artist, while a clever journeyman or apprentice executed the frames or borders which surround them, the architectural pieces, and other ornaments of the like kind.

We will now proceed to examine the Pompeian paintings with regard to the place which they should occupy considered as works of art.

Although the wall-paintings of Pompeii are almost the only ones that can convey to us any idea of Greek art, it must at the same time be regarded as a very imperfect idea. They are the productions only of a small provincial town, and that, too, at a period when the art of painting was already on the decline. Nevertheless, after making these allowances, they have served not only to correct, but also to elevate, our ideas of ancient painting, as is evident from a comparison of what has been written on that subject before and after their discovery; and it is now pretty generally allowed that both with regard to subject, composition, drawing, and colouring, it is of a higher grade than had been previously supposed.

Allowance must further be made for the circumstance that Pompeian painting, in the mass, can be regarded only as *decorative* painting. The larger mythological compositions and the pictures of domestic life, or *genre* pictures, might indeed by some be regarded as specimens of a higher and more substantial kind of art, and as having a loftier ideal character. In support of this view it might be urged that the painted frames which surround these compositions and separate them from the other wall decorations, as well as the circumstance that some of them are let into the walls, tend to show that they are pictures, in the stricter sense of the word, as opposed to mere decorations. And it appears to us that if they can be shown to have been copies, or even free imitations, of paintings by celebrated masters, as we think some of them undoubtedly were, this circumstance must also tend to add to their ideal character. As a general remark, however, it is no doubt true that the wall-paintings of Pompeii are essentially decorative, and thus even the pictures of a better and higher class would be made subservient to this purpose. Hence we may account for exaggerated voluptuousness, frequent hastiness of execution, and other defects. At the same time, regarding them in this decorative character, we must not overlook their excellent adaptation to the purpose intended; the cheerfulness and airiness which counteracted the darkness and narrowness of their framing; the inexhaustible wealth of ornament; the good selection and suitable grouping of objects; the excellent adaptation of the ornaments to the size and purposes of the room, by making them sometimes richer, sometimes simpler, now in darker colours, now in lighter, and the harmony in the general aspect of an apartment painted in this manner. Even the circle of subjects chosen for the greater pictures may be regarded as subsidiary to the main object of decoration. Although confined to a small sphere, it offers, nevertheless, a great variety, and embraces only those myths, which, through their frequent treatment by poets and artists, had become the common property of the educated world. They are of a familiar kind, and calculated to excite gentle and pleasurable emotions without the trouble of much thought or study, and were thus admirably adapted for rooms which were to serve as daily habitations. In the same manner the predominance of subjects which charm and delight the senses, rather than those which excite sublime or tragical emotions, must be regarded as in no small degree connected with the essentially decorative character of these paintings.

Besides the allowances which, on the preceding grounds, are to be made when viewing the paintings of Pompeii as samples of ancient art, we must also consider the circumstances under which they are seen. Those that have been removed to the National Museum are not only out of place and separated from their proper accompaniments, but have also been frequently put in situations where they can scarcely be seen, or, at all events, can be seen only very imperfectly. They have, moreover, been badly treated, and some of them have been repeatedly daubed with varnish, so as hardly to be recognized any longer. Their colours also have faded and changed, the natural effect of atmospheric and other influences during a period of many centuries. Of late days a better plan has been adopted of leaving the pictures just as they were found, where they will be better studied and understood. But even in their original situations we must remember that there are still some allowances to be made; and especially that they are viewed under a quite different light. For the houses being now uncovered, they are seen in broad day and sunshine, for which few or none were originally calculated; since even those in the atriums and peristyles were seen in a comparatively broken light. In some of the smaller and darker rooms it is difficult to say how the light could have penetrated at all. In such rooms the pictures must sometimes have been hardly visible except by lamp or candle light. The Pantheon is perhaps the best place in which to judge of the effects originally intended. On the left of the entrance the paintings are covered with a broad roof, and in this situation their colours appear more fresh and lively.

The Pompeian paintings, with regard to their subjects, may be divided

o

into the four following classes: first, architectural and other decorative painting; second, landscape, with more or fewer figures; third, *genre* pictures, or
scenes from familiar life and from the drama, including also still life, fruit,
flowers, &c; fourth, historical painting.

The first of these classes, in its lower kinds, cannot properly be called
artistic painting; it rather resembles the work of our higher sort of house
painters; such as the representation of various coloured marbles, socles, cor-
nices, pillars, &c. Artistic painting may, however, be said to begin with the fantastic architectural views and perspectives which form a sort of frame for other
pictures; as in the photograph of the wall of Sirieus given above. To enter
into all the varieties of this sort of architectural decoration would require
many pages of description, which even then would not convey so lively and
accurate an idea of it as the inspection of a few walls, or of the pictures of
them in the works of Gell, Niccolini, Zahn, and others. Perhaps one of the
most perfect specimens of wall-painting at Pompeii is that in the House of
the Toilette of Hermaphroditus, which will be found beautifully represented
in the last-named writer's "Ornamente aller classischen Kunstepochen,"
Heft xvii. taf. 81. It will suffice here to say that this kind of painting
varies from a couple of small pillars, or a view into a neighbouring room, up
to buildings of several stories, with stairs, balconies, porticos, and aerial
perspectives. These architectural decorations, or frames, vary in richness
according to the objects which they enclose. The most simple ones enclose
only a portion of the painted wall, either quite plain or with only an insig-
nificant design or figure upon it; others, growing richer in proportion, contain
medallions, pieces of landscape or still life, and so up to the mythological
pictures. The socles and friezes are also adorned with small figures wherever
there is space, as genii, cupids, and other children.

The second sort of paintings—namely, landscapes with more or fewer
figures,—are found either in the socles and friezes, or in the middle compartments of the wall; varying, of course, in size and importance according to the
place which they occupy, and also, it is hardly necessary to say, in the
manner in which they are treated. The small and less important consist
merely of a few bushes, or a tree, near which some animal is grazing.
Others present a building and a tree or two, with a distant prospect over sea,
or plain, or mountain. Some consist of a sea piece, perhaps, with a ship near
an island or tongue of land, on which is a temple or a portico. These are
varied with a few figures, as a shepherd or two with some animals. Some-

times they are of a comical nature, as in a little picture in which is seen a part of the banks of the Nile. A donkey, with a pannier on its back, is going to drink without noticing a lurking crocodile, into whose jaws it is running, whilst the driver is straining every muscle to pull him back by the tail. Larger pictures are essentially views, with architectural perspectives of fantastic buildings, bridges, harbours, temples, porticos, and even whole quarters of towns; or of a more rural character, where trees and bushes are more numerous than the buildings. Such views are peopled with figures of promenaders, shepherds, fishermen with rods or nets, sailors rowing or sailing, sacrificers, travellers in coaches or on donkeys, fowlers, hunters, persons engaged in the vintage, &c. One Ludius is said to have introduced this sort of wall-painting in the time of Augustus (Plin. *N. H.*, xxxv. 116 sq.) The annexed cut will convey some notion of this sort of picture. A few of such landscapes occupy a space of eight or ten feet square; but these are very rare instances. Sometimes, but rarely, such pictures contain figures representing a mythological subject, but which are evidently subordinate to the landscape. One of these, for instance, represents Perseus delivering Andromeda from the sea-monster. The figures here are seen in the sea, in the foreground, while

FARM-YARD SCENE.

behind is a rocky and desolate coast, on which the waves are breaking, and where the aspect of desolation is augmented by several dead trees which are seen in the middle distance.

The third class of painting, which may be called *genre* painting, or representations of domestic or familiar life, must be taken in a very extensive signification, so as to embrace all those objects which cannot be included in the definition either of landscape painting or of mythological and historical painting.

The lowest class of pictures of this class are those representing still life—as dead game, fish, flowers, fruit, &c; and it may be remarked that the representations of eatables are much more numerous than those of any other objects.

The *renationes*, or combats with beasts in the amphitheatre, naturally suggested the paintings of animals with which several of the houses at Pompeii are adorned; though in such cases they are not represented in the amphitheatre, but in some wild landscape suitable to their savage nature. Some of these are executed with a great deal of spirit; but on the whole they are not to be compared to some modern efforts in this style.

Of *genre* paintings, in which the human figure is introduced, we must place in the lowest class those in which no story is told, but consist of one or two figures, or even mere heads in medallion, or otherwise. Such are the flying figures so frequently seen on the walls, and medallions like those of Mars and Venus in the House of the Rudder and Trident, called also, from

these paintings, *Casa di Marte e Venere*. Of the same kind are a remarkable series of eight small pictures in a bed-room in the House of Holconius, representing in square compartments the usual personages of the Bacchic thiasos. Thus one of the compartments shows Bacchus himself, another, Ariadne, others, Bacchantes and Fauns, Paris with his crook and Phrygian cap, &c. The annexed photograph of Bacchus and a Faun will convey an idea of this sort of painting. The figures, so frequently recurring on the walls, of dancing women are also commonly called Bacchantes; but according to more modern inquirers this is a mistake. They are mere human dancers, perhaps, belonging to the lowest classes of society, executing some of the mimic dances of antiquity. Some of the best specimens of this sort were found at an early period in a house near the Gate of Herculaneum, called, after them, *Casa delle Danzatrici*. One of these figures is represented in the accompanying cut.

FIGURE IN THE HOUSE OF THE FEMALE DANCERS.

FRESCO OF BACCHUS AND FAUN.

Paintings with a few figures representing some scene of ordinary life are such as that, to which we have already alluded in the House of the Fuller, representing the process of cleaning or fulling cloth, of a female painter copying a head of Bacchus, while two other women look on, and others of the like kind. Some of these are of a grotesque and comical character, resembling our caricature, as one found in the *Casa Carolina,* and represented in the following cut. A pigmy artist, somewhat scantily

STUDIO OF A PAINTER OF ANTIQUITY.

dressed, is taking the portrait of another pigmy, whose head already makes a great figure upon the canvas. The distance at which the artist sits from his work, and the manner in which he holds the brush, seem to demand great steadiness and sureness of hand, and suggest the notion that some practice of this sort was requisite in order to obtain that certainty of touch which the wall-painting must have demanded. The easel much resembles our own, while by the artist's side is a little table with his palette and a pot in which to wash his brushes. On the right his colour-grinder is preparing colours mixed with wax and oil in a vessel with hot embers under it. In the distance is a pupil, who, disturbed apparently by the entrance of two amateurs, turns round to see what is going forward. The visitors seem to be discussing the merits of the picture. At the extremity is a bird, the meaning of which is not obvious, but is supposed to typify some singer or musician.

The representation of little cupids, or winged genii, engaged in various occupations, is a very favourite subject for paintings of this kind; and it must be allowed that their forms and attitudes are generally rendered with great elegance and playfulness. They are depicted hunting, fishing, dancing, playing, and sometimes engaged in very commonplace and mechanical occupations. Thus in one picture two of these little figures are represented as carpenters sawing a board; in another, as shoemakers engaged upon their trade at a table, while on shelves round the room are several specimens of their handiwork ready for sale. They are, of course, more frequently found in their proper capacity as messengers of love, and engaged in all sorts of *espiégleries* in the service of the ladies. A favourite subject of this sort is the love-merchant—an old man who offers to some fair one a cage full of loves for sale. Among the wall-paintings of Pompeii are two or three celebrated pictures of this kind. In one of these a handsome lady is leaning against a pillar. On the ground before her is a cage, out of which an old man is pulling a little Cupid by the wing, while two more still remain in it. Two have been previously released, one of whom has hid himself behind the lady and peeps forth to see what the old man is doing; while a fifth, on whom the lady's gaze is intently fixed—and perhaps this little love is the right one—is flying towards her with two garlands in his hands. In all this there was doubtless a hidden meaning at which we can only guess.

A still more elevated class of *genre* pictures are those representing scenes from the drama, either tragic or comic. The first of these kinds comes more properly under that higher class of painting which we reserve for final examination, and we shall have to advert again to some of these tragic scenes: we mention them here in conjunction with the comic scenes, for the sake of convenience, and because they are both representations of theatrical rather than real life; if the epithet *real* may be applied to mythological and epic subjects. Such scenes were, no doubt, taken from well-known and popular plays, and, like the mythological subjects, would be familiar to every

educated person. We insert a cut of either kind, as they will serve to show the different costumes of tragedy and comedy. In the first, or tragic scene, will be observed the ὄγκος, or lofty wig, and the *cothurni*, buskins, or high shoes, employed to increase the actors' stature. To add in proportion to the other parts of the figure, the body was stuffed and padded, and the arms were lengthened by means of gloves, so as to convey

TRAGIC SCENE, FROM A PAINTING AT POMPEII.

the idea of colossal and super-human size. Such additions, as well as the

exaggerated features of the masks, seem to have been rendered necessary by
the vast size of the ancient theatres;
to our taste, at least, nothing but
the softening effects of distance
could have rendered such pre-
posterous figures endurable. In
comedy a more natural character
was preserved, as will be seen
from the second cut.

COMIC SCENE, FROM A PAINTING AT POMPEII.

We now approach the higher
class of painting, which had for its
subjects the gods and heroes of mythology. Here also we may observe two
distinct classes; namely, pictures which tell no story, but which consist of
single figures, or, at most, two or three not engaged in any particular action;
and another and a higher kind,
which represent some well-known
mythological, epic, or tragic story.

The single figures represented
in this sort of painting are principally those of the gods, accompanied in general with their attributes. The house at the top of
the Street of Mercury, near the
triumphal arch, called sometimes
the *Casa del Naviglio*, or House of
the Ship, sometimes also of Zephyrus and Flora, or of Ceres,
contained in its atrium several
fine paintings of this sort; as
Jupiter, Bacchus, Cybele, Ceres,
and Mercury, in sitting postures.
Some of these have been carried
to the Museum, others have become effaced or nearly so. We
insert a cut of one of the latter,
representing Jupiter enthroned, in
a contemplative attitude. At his

PAINTING OF JUPITER, FROM THE HOUSE OF CERES.

feet is the eagle; his head, which is surrounded with a *nimbus*, or glory, rests upon his right hand, while in his left he holds a golden sceptre. The throne, partly covered with green cloth, and the footstool were also of gold, adorned with precious stones; his mantle was of a violet colour, lined with azure. These higher gods, from motives of reverential piety, which will be easily conceived, were seldom represented in action. These paintings, in conjunction with statues, help us to an idea of the forms and attributes with which the ancients endowed their deities. The House of the Quæstor, or of Castor and Pollux, in the same street, contained a noble painting of Ceres, esteemed the most important representation of that goddess to be found in the whole circle of ancient art.

Both these houses, as well as many others, contain flying figures of mythological personages. For these representations such gods and goddesses, or demi-gods, were naturally chosen, in whom the act of hovering in the air did not seem unnatural, or incompatible with their dignity. A flying Jupiter, or Juno, or Minerva, would be intolerable, while such an act appears a natural and even graceful one in an Iris or Aurora, a Victoria or a Hebe. In the same category may be placed most of the personages of the Bacchic troop, Bacchantes, Mænades, Centaurs, and the like. Such figures do not occupy the centre compartment or post of honour in a wall, but are used to adorn the side divisions. In the same class may be placed quiescent figures, as Muses, or allegorical figures representing Poetry, Music, Peace, and the like.

We come now to the highest class of paintings, or those in which some mythological or epic story is represented. Pictures of this class demand, of course, for their proper execution the highest talents of an artist, not only in the more mechanical parts of drawing and colouring, grouping and composition, but also as to the manner in which the story is told, the beauty and dignity of the figures, and the passions expressed in their attitudes and features.

With regard only to the mechanical handling, these ancient pictures, though far from being the mere statuesque representations which they were once thought to be, yet differ very widely from modern art. One of the widest of these differences lies in the way in which the light is managed. They present none of those striking effects of light and shade so often seen in modern pictures, and which it must be confessed are sometimes little better than tricks of art, by throwing the light through an open door, or window, or some similar artifice. All the Pompeian paintings are what may be called *day-light* pictures. In none of them, except one recently found, supposed to represent the matricide of Alcmæon, do the persons represented throw a shadow on the ground. The light in the Pompeian pictures, with perhaps one or two exceptions, is so clear and regularly distributed as to give them a certain air of coldness. Yet, from the accounts of ancient writers, we may conclude that ancient painting was not deficient in effects of light and shade; and we may therefore, perhaps, with Overbeck, attribute the style observable in the Pompeian pictures to the circumstance that they were intended to decorate rooms not over well lighted, and in which, consequently, pictures with much shadow in them would have produced but little effect; while, on the other hand, the dark grounds of the walls in which they were inserted served to bring out the colouring of the figures. As we do not now see them under the light for which they were designed, we are hardly competent to pronounce an opinion upon them with regard to this point.

It must likewise be considered that the colouring of these ancient frescos, like modern pictures of the same kind, could not possess the warmth and glow of an oil-painting. On the other hand, pleasing and striking effects are often produced in them by a contrast of colours; as, for instance, in the picture of the education of Achilles, the contrast of the light and brilliant carnations of the youthful hero's skin with the tawny red of that of the Centaur. The same effect is observable in the flying figures of Bacchants and Bacchantes, and also in the contrast of skin and clothing. And on the whole the colouring of the larger pictures must be pronounced harmonious. Colours are seldom or never found in combination which produce a disagreeable effect upon the eye; nor, however highly coloured a picture may be, is it ever spotty or patchy. The drawing is often incorrect, but seldom wanting in vigour; it more frequently falls perhaps into the opposite fault of exaggeration.

Even the larger pictures differ, of course, very much among themselves with regard to the composition and grouping. Some consist of only a few figures, in which there is little story to be told, while others contain a great many, and represent an action of the most touching and interesting kind. Of the former class are such pictures as that already mentioned of the Centaur instructing Achilles, Meleager returned from hunting, Narcissus viewing himself in the fountain, &c, and most of those of an amatory kind;

P

as the loves of Mars and Venus, of Venus and Adonis, of Diana and Endymion, &c.   The annexed photograph, from a picture of Mars and Venus, will convey an idea how such subjects are treated.   Some pictures, on the other hand, from the interest attaching to the story represented, and the emotions which it is calculated to excite, demand the very highest powers of a painter. Such, for instance, is the celebrated painting of Achilles dismissing Briseis; perhaps, on the whole, the finest discovered at Pompeii, and calculated, had it been the only one, to give us a very high idea of ancient art.   It was found in the House of the Tragic Poet, excavated in 1824.   Achilles is sitting enthroned before his tent; his shield leans against the side of the throne; in his left hand he lightly holds a sceptre, with the right he gives the signal for the delivery of Briseis to Agamemnon's heralds.   Nothing can surpass the dignity and grace of the figure of Achilles.   The head is a perfect model of youthful manly beauty; the countenance expresses both love and anger as he fixes his eyes on the lovely Briseis, and revolves in his mind the tyrannical act of Agamemnon; while the nudity of the upper part of the body gives full scope for the display of his fine muscular development.   An idea of this head may be obtained from Sir W. Gell's " Pompeiana" (second series); but a better one from Ternite's " Wandgemälde von Pompeji," with explanatory letter-press by C. O. Müller.   Gell's engraving was taken from a sketch by Ternite, and is said by him not to do it justice.   We borrow the following description of this celebrated picture from Sir W. Gell:—

" The scene seems to take place in the tent of Achilles, who sits in the centre.   Patroclus, with his back towards the spectator, and with a skin of deeper red, leads in from the left the lovely Briseis, arrayed in a long and floating veil of apple-green.   Her face is beautiful, and not to dwell upon the archness of her eye, it is evident that the voluptuous pouting of her ruby lip was imagined by the painter as one of her most bewitching attributes.   Achilles presents the fair one to the heralds on his right; and his attitude, his manly beauty, and the magnificent expression of his countenance are inimitable.

" The tent seems to be divided by a drapery about breast high, and of a sort of dark bluish green, like the tent itself.   Behind this stand several warriors, the golden shield of one of whom, whether intentionally or not on the part of the painter, forms a sort of glory round the head of the principal hero.

" It is probably the copy of one of the most celebrated pictures of antiquity.

FRESCO OF MARS AND VENUS.

" When first discovered the colours were fresh, and the flesh particularly had the transparency of Titian. It suffered much and unavoidably during the excavation, and something from the means taken to preserve it, when a committee of persons qualified to judge had decided that the wall on which it was painted, was not in a state to admit of its removal with safety. At length, after an exposure of more than two years, it was thought better to attempt to transport it to the studii at Naples, than to suffer it entirely to disappear from the wall. It was accordingly removed with success in the summer of the year 1826, and it is hoped that some remains of it may exist for posterity.

" The painter has chosen the moment when the heralds, Talthybius and Eurybates, are put in possession of Briseis, to escort her to the tent of Agamemnon, as described in the first book of the Iliad, and thus translated by Pope:—

> Patroclus now th' unwilling beauty brought ;
> She in soft sorrow and in pensive thought
> Passed silent, as the heralds held her hand,
> And oft looked back, slow moving o'er the sand."

The size of this picture was four feet two inches by four feet.

Another famous picture, and requiring, for an adequate representation of the subject, the highest powers of art, was that of Medea meditating the murder of her children; forming one of the paintings in the House of the Quæstor. Like a few other of the Pompeian pictures, it is supposed to have been a copy of a Greek master-piece; and in this instance the prototype is said to have been the celebrated work on the same subject by Timomachus of Byzantium. This picture, with another of Ajax, by the same artist, were purchased by Julius Cæsar for the enormous sum of eighty Attic talents, or between £19,000 and £20,000, in order to adorn his temple of Venus Genitrix. It seems probable that the picture of Timomachus contained only the figure of Medea, and that the children did not appear, or were, at all events, treated in a very subordinate manner. The painter relied—as only a great artist could—on the effect to be produced by the expression of Medea, before she had yet quite resolved upon the dreadful act, and while the emotions of maternal love for her children and revenge against the father of them are still struggling for the mastery. It is, indeed, in this struggle, more than in the act itself, that the tragic interest of the story lies; and Timomachus, in a different art, only followed the principles of the Greek drama in keeping the actual murder out of sight, in accord with Horace's well-known line :—

Nec pueros coram populo Medea trucidet.

The sword yet remained undrawn in her folded hands, but her lingering, irresolute attitude, and her speaking features, told the whole story. The work of Timomachus could therefore have only suggested the general idea to the painter of the Pompeian picture; for though, in the latter, the head and attitude of Medea appear to bear considerable resemblance to the picture of Timomachus, yet she is already beginning to draw her sword. This alteration, however, may perhaps be justified on the ground that in the Pompeian picture the children are introduced; whose careless innocence while engaged in a game of dice or marbles, and totally unconscious of the fate that hangs over them, is a touching feature in the composition. Yet it would lose much of its effect unless the spectator saw, both by the action of Medea and the horror expressed in the countenance and attitude of the children's pedagogue, that their death was resolved on.

We shall mention only one more picture of this kind,—the Sacrifice of Iphigenia, in the House of the Tragic Poet. This also is thought to be a copy of the celebrated picture of Timanthes on the same subject; and it is, at all events, certain that it contains a characteristic feature of the Greek original,—the veiled head of Agamemnon. It is singular that Pliny and Quintilian, who must have been acquainted with the Medea of Timomachus, should have thought that Timanthes adopted this attitude from inability to portray the expression of sorrow in the features of Agamemnon. The loss that he was called on to endure was no doubt heart-rending enough; but the sacrifice of a daughter at the call of religion, and by its ministers, can hardly be compared to the agony of Medea, agitated by opposite and contending passions, and about to murder her children with her own hand. Yet Timomachus was able to express the intensity of that agony with a skill that excited universal admiration. After all that has been written on this question, we may find a simple solution of it in the natural custom of concealing our sorrow and our tears; and, perhaps, the artist could have chosen no better method to awaken the sympathy of the spectators with the grief of a father and a king. The picture represents the moment at which Chalcas is about to strike the fatal blow. Iphigenia, borne away by two men, is appealing to her father; but, by some defect in the drawing, she

FRESCO OF JUDGMENT OF PARIS.

appears to have no legs; for it is quite impossible to imagine that they could have been altogether hidden behind one of her supporters. To the left, on a small pillar, is seen a golden image of Diana, with two dogs at her feet, and a lighted torch in each hand. The goddess herself appears in the clouds, while another female figure is bringing the hind which is to be substituted for Iphigenia as a victim.

The three preceding pictures are taken from the heroic cycle, which afforded a much greater quantity of subjects to the artists of Pompeii than the history and adventures of the gods of Olympus. Subjects of the latter kind are not, however, wanting. They are generally love scenes: as the amours of Jupiter with Leda and Danae, the abduction of Ganymede, the pursuit of Daphne by Apollo, the loves of Mars and Venus, of Venus and Adonis, of Luna and Endymion, of Mercury and Herse, of Zephyrus and Flora, &c. The judgment of Paris seems to have been a favourite subject, and is often repeated. The accompanying photograph is a specimen of its manner of treatment. But Bacchus affords more subjects than any other deity, his story and worship being rich in picturesque materials. Such are his education when a child by old Silenus, scenes from his vagrant ramblings with his chorus of Satyrs and Bacchantes, his invention of the drama, and more frequently than any, his discovery of Ariadne abandoned by Theseus: of which last we have already given a specimen.

In like manner, the subjects taken from the heroic cycle commonly turn upon love adventures, and serious or tragic scenes are comparatively rare; a circumstance which, as before explained, may be referred to the essentially decorative character of these paintings. For, when the eye is to dwell habitually on them, pleasing scenes of this description are preferable to those which awaken painful emotions. The three pictures, indeed, before described, are of a serious, and two of them of a highly tragic nature. But these are exceptions to the general practice, and they were selected merely as instances of the skill and power with which the ancient painters could treat the most elevated and pathetic subjects.

From the heroic cycle, the labours of Hercules, the adventures of Theseus, the Argonautic expedition, and the hunting of the Calydonian boar, furnish the most numerous subjects. Of all the labours of Hercules, his combat with the Nemean lion is that most frequently selected for representation. It is found not only in pictures, but also on vases, gems, and coins. From the life of Theseus, we find the recovery of his father's arms, his victory over the Minotaur in the Cretan Labyrinth, and, what is very frequently repeated, his abandonment of the sleeping Ariadne at Naxos. From the legend of the Argonauts, besides the story of Medea already mentioned, we find that of Phrixus and Helle, and the landing of the former at Æa. Perseus and Andromeda is a favourite subject, and his exhibiting to her in a fountain the head of Medusa. We have also Meleager returned from hunting, Meleager and Atalanta, &c. Scenes from the Trojan War, and the events which preceded and followed it, are, of course, of frequent recurrence. Of the judgment of Paris we have already given an example. We find besides, Leda with the nest, containing the Dioscuri and Helen, Apollo and Neptune building the walls of Troy, Thetis dipping Achilles in the Styx, his education by the Centaur Chiron, his discovery by Ulysses among the daughters of Lycomedes, Thetis receiving Achilles' arms from Vulcan, his dismissal of Briseïs (in a picture already mentioned), &c. Pictures of events that occurred after the fall of Troy are not so common; but we have from the Odyssey, Ulysses and Circe (a picture in the house of Modestus, already mentioned), and in the so-called Pantheon, a charming picture of the interview of Ulysses with Penelope when he returns to his home in the disguise of a beggar.

It will be observed that all the preceding examples are drawn from Greek sources, while those which can be traced to an Italian or Latin origin are exceedingly rare indeed. This fact serves to confirm the idea that the paintings of Pompeii were the work of Greek artists, and that they were copies, or, at all events, more or less free imitations of Greek originals. Fiorelli,* indeed, in two paintings recently discovered in the house of Siricus, or Salve Lucrum, thinks that he can recognize subjects taken from the *Æneid.* The first is thought to represent Iapis operating upon the wound of Æneas; the second, Turnus between Lavinia and Amata, when the latter dissuades him from again fighting with the Trojans. These explanations, however, and especially as regards the latter picture, are very problematical. But representations of Romulus and Remus suckled by the wolf, of Vesta and the Lares, and one or two other Roman subjects are occasionally found.

Of the art of antiquity, mosaic, next to painting, has been most illustrated by the discoveries at Pompeii; for though some exquisite little statuettes have been found, especially the well-known ones of the Dancing

---

* "Giornale degli Scavi." No. xiii. p. 17. sq.

Faun, the Silenus, and the Narcissus, yet in this branch of art the remains discovered at Pompeii are but small in comparison with the vast treasures of sculpture collected from other quarters.

Mosaic, or the art of inlaying in various coloured stones, was at first only employed in pavements, and consisted of a few simple patterns. By degrees, and under the successors of Alexander, it obtained a higher development, and began, by the representation of objects, to emulate painting. The first eminent artist in this way whom we find mentioned is Sosus of Pergamus; who in one of his pieces imitated the unswept floor of a dining room, with a vessel full of water on it, upon the sides of which were a dove drinking, and others sunning themselves. Copies of this celebrated work have been found at Hadrian's Villa near Tivoli, and at Naples. The materials of this art at first consisted of pieces of stone, marble, or coloured clay; at a later period, even precious stones were used, and at last coloured glass, as at present. At Pompeii this art was employed not only for floors, but also for wall-paintings—of which there is a specimen in the House of Apollo —and even for the decoration of columns. Many fine specimens were discovered there, among which may be mentioned two bearing the name of Dioscorides, and representing comic scenes. The House of the Faun was particularly rich in mosaics. Here were found a beautiful border on the threshold of the atrium, consisting of masks, wreaths, &c. considered to be one of the finest specimens of decorative mosaic. Also, in one of the rooms of the same house, the pretty design of Acratus riding on a panther; but, above all, the celebrated Battle of Issus, the largest and finest mosaic in the world, though unfortunately much damaged. Its situation in the National Museum does not allow a photograph of it to be taken, and as its subject could not be well explained without an engraving, we forbear to enter into it.

CHISWICK PRESS:—PRINTED BY WHITTINGHAM AND WILKINS,
TOOKS COURT, CHANCERY LANE.

Trieste

Trieste Publishing has a massive catalogue of classic book titles. Our aim is to provide readers with the highest quality reproductions of fiction and non-fiction literature that has stood the test of time. The many thousands of books in our collection have been sourced from libraries and private collections around the world.

The titles that Trieste Publishing has chosen to be part of the collection have been scanned to simulate the original. Our readers see the books the same way that their first readers did decades or a hundred or more years ago. Books from that period are often spoiled by imperfections that did not exist in the original. Imperfections could be in the form of blurred text, photographs, or missing pages. It is highly unlikely that this would occur with one of our books. Our extensive quality control ensures that the readers of Trieste Publishing's books will be delighted with their purchase. Our staff has thoroughly reviewed every page of all the books in the collection, repairing, or if necessary, rejecting titles that are not of the highest quality. This process ensures that the reader of one of Trieste Publishing's titles receives a volume that faithfully reproduces the original, and to the maximum degree possible, gives them the experience of owning the original work.

We pride ourselves on not only creating a pathway to an extensive reservoir of books of the finest quality, but also providing value to every one of our readers. Generally, Trieste books are purchased singly - on demand, however they may also be purchased in bulk. Readers interested in bulk purchases are invited to contact us directly to enquire about our tailored bulk rates. Email: customerservice@triestepublishing.com

You May Also Like

ISBN: 9780649203536
Paperback: 210 pages
Dimensions: 6.14 x 0.44 x 9.21 inches
Language: eng

**Negro life in the South, present conditions and needs.
With a special chapter on the economic condition of the negro**

Willis D. Weatherford & G. W Dyer

ISBN: 9780649184927
Paperback: 208 pages
Dimensions: 6.14 x 0.44 x 9.21 inches
Language: eng

A life for God in India: memorials of Mrs. Jennie Fuller of Akola and Bombay

Helen S. Dyer

www.triestepublishing.com

You May Also Like

History of the battle of Lake Erie, and miscellaneous papers

George Bancroft & Oliver Dyer

ISBN: 9780649163045
Paperback: 294 pages
Dimensions: 6.14 x 0.62 x 9.21 inches
Language: eng

The Celestial and his religions: or, The religious aspect in China. Being a series of lectures on the religions of the Chinese

J. Dyer Ball

ISBN: 9780649117734
Paperback: 276 pages
Dimensions: 6.14 x 0.58 x 9.21 inches
Language: eng

www.triestepublishing.com

You May Also Like

Haym Salomon: The Financier of the Revolution : an Unwritten Chapter in American History

Madison C. Peters

ISBN: 9781760570170
Paperback: 56 pages
Dimensions: 6.14 x 0.12 x 9.21 inches
Language: eng

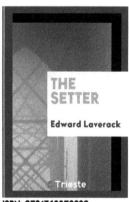

The setter

Edward Laverack

ISBN: 9781760570309
Paperback: 90 pages
Dimensions: 6.14 x 0.19 x 9.21 inches
Language: eng

www.triestepublishing.com

You May Also Like

The Ship Captain's Medical Guide

Harry Leach

ISBN: 9781760570620
Paperback: 120 pages
Dimensions: 6.14 x 0.25 x 9.21 inches
Language: eng

Around the Year in Rhymes for the Jewish Child

Jessie E. Sampter

ISBN: 9781760570712
Paperback: 104 pages
Dimensions: 5.83 x 0.22 x 8.27 inches
Language: eng

Find more of our titles on our website. We have a selection of thousands of titles that will interest you. Please visit

www.triestepublishing.com

Lightning Source UK Ltd.
Milton Keynes UK
UKHW02f1013010618
323578UK00004B/300/P

9 780649 136575